Awakening

TO THE POWER OF INTUITION

T0116811

Awakening

TO THE POWER OF INTUITION

LEARN TWENTY-EIGHT LESSONS
TO CHANGE YOUR LIFE

Anita Martin

BALBOA.
PRESS

A DIVISION OF HAY HOUSE

Balboa Press books may be ordered through booksellers or by contacting:

Balboa Press
A Division of Hay House
1663 Liberty Drive
Bloomington, IN 47403
www.balboapress.com
1-(877) 407-4847

Because of the dynamic nature of the Internet, any web addresses or
links contained in this book may have changed since publication and
may no longer be valid. The views expressed in this work are solely those
of the author and do not necessarily reflect the views of the publisher,
and the publisher hereby disclaims any responsibility for them.

The author of this book does not dispense medical advice or prescribe the use
of any technique as a form of treatment for physical, emotional, or medical
problems without the advice of a physician, either directly or indirectly. The
intent of the author is only to offer information of a general nature to help
you in your quest for emotional and spiritual well-being. In the event you use
any of the information in this book for yourself, which is your constitutional
right, the author and the publisher assume no responsibility for your actions.

Any people depicted in stock imagery provided by Thinkstock are
models, and such images are being used for illustrative purposes only.
Certain stock imagery © Thinkstock.

ISBN: 978-1-4525-3968-3 (sc)
ISBN: 978-1-4525-3969-0 (hc)
ISBN: 978-1-4525-3970-6 (e)

Library of Congress Control Number: 2011917318

Printed in the United States of America

Balboa Press rev. date: 10/21/2011

'Too many doubt their own potential and never try to achieve their dream, because they have been damaged by bad thought patterns. Allowing myself to be free to 'experience' was giving me permission to rebel from the 'normality of middle age'. It was a huge awakening and women everywhere were asking 'Don't you feel lonely?' Surprisingly, I didn't!'

Anita Martin

CONTENTS

ACKNOWLEDGEMENTS

My intuition has led me to value myself and I have always felt that if we value ourselves we will be surrounded by others that value us too. Consequently I am now surrounded by truly wonderful people.

First I would like to thank Linda who was truly supportive when I decided to embark on this journey of a lifetime. Linda not only accompanied me to Heathrow Airport but also returned to collect me at the end of my adventure. When I first started my business in 2000 synchronicities really kicked in when Linda and I met. We soon realised that we both recognised in each other something we were both asking for. Linda was searching for spiritual awakening and I needed a computer whizz kid to help me with technology. A special friendship developed and has remained between us.

Another person who I am truly grateful to is Sue, a dear friend and work colleague, who has not only become truly supportive of all my work but has also invested many hours in assisting me in getting this book presentable for publication. Sue and I met as co trainers and soon realised we shared many views and made a good team in working together and also supporting each other in our individual roles. I look forward to us working together long into the future.

I would like to thank all those I've met on my courses over the years working as a trainer, who have given me so much insight into their lives and have dared to share intimate details. Without knowing what others experience how would I know the value of what I teach? The courage and determination of individuals has never ceased to amaze me and continues to teach me new lessons on just how powerful we all are when we learn to listen to our intuition.

Thank you to all those I met in New Zealand, especially Wendy who welcomed me into her home and supported me when I needed a guiding hand. She truly showed me how intuition really does lead us where we are meant to go and it was lovely to return to her at the end of my travels and share my amazing journey.

INTRODUCTION

What is intuition?

It was once described to me by a student as a *knowing*.

So what is this 6th sense that we possess but so often don't use and why isn't it given the same attention that our other senses are?

If our eyes did not see, or ears didn't hear or our tongues couldn't taste or noses didn't smell or even if our skin couldn't feel, we would at least investigate why, wouldn't we?

Yet, amazingly we do not question whether our intuition is working or not and yet it is one of our senses.

Of course I am aware this applies mostly to the Western world, as it would be quite different in a lot of the Eastern countries, where they naturally use their intuition all the time.

Though if we were to step back in time even in a Western country, before technology was so advanced, using intuition was a natural way of living. People were encouraged to use their 6th sense far more as they couldn't relay on electronic machines to give them the solutions to everything. Of course it may not have

been identified as intuition, more just doing what felt right.

Intuition is often linked to our 3rd eye, located on our forehead between both our eyes and is commonly known as a 'gut' feeling.

Healthy babies are born with all of their senses including intuition. Totally open to what the universe has to offer, trusting in those who show love and attention.

They accept and respond to all that happens around them and only need to be loved and cared for. They have no fear or judgment and no thoughts of yesterday or tomorrow. Their only concern is of what is happening 'now'. As they grow they will become small children who move naturally and think without analyzing, being totally aware and sensing energies around them. We can witness this by observing the way an infant reacts to the moods of those close to them.

They are naturally intuitive and this only diminishes as they grow older because of adult intervention from planting fear into their tender minds. How sad that we are so often stripped of the most valuable lesson of all, at such a tender age and then spend the rest of our life searching for the very thing we lost, our 'intuition'.

A child focuses so well on what's happening right in front of them, aware of the finest detail. Ask a magician who his most difficult audience is and he will tell you 'children' as they have not lost the ability to 'see beyond'.

Our intuition is a wonderful sense and if nurtured can help guide us through our most difficult and darkest hours. Having worked with so many people who wanted to discover the power of their

own intuition I have been constantly enriched through witnessing their personal growth which comes as a result of daring to explore and practice using this very neglected sense.

My journey with intuition has been a truly amazing one and as a result I am now able to welcome change into my life without fear, as I know it is a natural part of my journey. I have made some wonderful connections along the way, some who are still around, others who have moved on, but I've come to understand that I'm not meant to know how long these connections are meant to be, another lesson that has truly freed me.

I believe that we come into each other's lives to learn lessons and maybe to stay around for a while, but not necessarily forever. In reality there is a lot of evidence that demonstrates how true this is, so why do we so often resist letting go of someone who evidently wants to let go of us? It would be far more empowering if we appreciated those we are privileged to spend some time with, without attaching ourselves too much. The reason we find ourselves trying so hard to hold on to someone else is often because we seek emotional attachment. Insecurity is often the cause of this. Sadly we often look for emotional fulfilment in another when really we need to be searching within ourselves. When we find it from within we are no longer needy and then will attract healthier relationships. Remember the saying 'Like attracts like'. Needy relationships so often end in tears as at least one of the partners will probably feel suffocated and then desire space and freedom, leaving their partner feeling desperate as fear of being alone is so often what started their neediness in the first place.

To truly love ourselves and feel secure in the knowing that we are being looked after by a love much greater than any human being can give, will give us the assurance that we don't need to seek it because it's already there within us.

So many people yearn to be rich, thinking that will solve all their problems and they would be happy for ever more, but I think deep down we know it doesn't work like that. If life was that easy then

I guess all the rich would be happy and the poor unhappy and we know that isn't true. So what is it about?

For me it's about finding truth and purpose and to discover why I am here. If and when we are lucky enough to discover these things, we can start living in an authentic way through the intention of our soul and not our ego, which unfortunately we so often feel pressured to respond to.

Sadly, acting on your ego alone will never bring you true happiness, but it will make you greedy and wanting more. Whereas living by your souls intention will lead to a fulfilled life. If you allow yourself quiet times to go within, your soul will talk to you and intuitively you will 'know' what is right for you to do. It may not be an easy choice but it will be the correct one. Your life will run smoother if you don't deny it by taking what feels like an easier route because the 'right one' felt difficult or uncomfortable. As you pursue the path you 'know' your life will run easier and you will be given the 'tools' and 'support' to deal with difficult situations.

True Connection

When two souls connect, they don't need to possess,

They are one, regardless of more or less.

To understand and accept another

Is a love known to a sister and brother.

However, to find a partner to share your life

Without necessarily being husband or wife,

But one who knows and respects your path

Who cries your tears and smiles when you laugh,

Listens to your words when you need to share

And gives you a hug to show they care,

One who has passion which you ignite

And together you know it feels so right.

That's a partner worth waiting for

And when they appear you'll want no more.

I have learned not to use energy in regretting the past, but instead to use the experience to identify the lesson and then learn from it and move forward.

Showing others who feel vulnerable, how to gain strength and avoid repeating the same lessons over and over again has been a very valuable part of my work as a personal development tutor and counsellor. However, I know from bitter experience that sometimes we do have to live through the same lessons with different people before we gain enough insight and strength to avoid them happening all over again.

On the following pages I will share with you my journey with intuition, including in chapter 3 my solo trip to New Zealand, when I documented each lesson that I identified along with my understanding and learning from it. I have then explored each lesson and what it could mean for all of us and invite you the reader to try the exercises for yourself.

By sharing my lessons with you I hope you will identify lessons in your own life and begin to recognize the messages they are giving you.

In order that you may use this book as a learning manual I have allowed space for you to add your own lessons, so you too may be able to explore what they mean for you.

DISCOVERING MY INTUITION

*'You get back what you give out' what I give out is what I attract in so
I will only give to others the love I want to receive back.*

Today I questioned . . . and dared to doubt. Why? Because I'm human!

I felt anxious, threatened, lonely and sad. I questioned so much . . . because I'm human!

We must never forget that we are human. A difficult lesson when we are developing spiritually, but one that constantly comes back to haunt us just when we thought we were growing so well.

It was a difficult day when my emotions felt raw and I felt tested on all levels, but I realised just how much I had grown when I knew despite all those negative feelings that were rushing through me I never doubted 'trust'. I knew all that was happening was for my higher good and all would be revealed when the time was right. How did I know? I guess this is how I identified my intuition. Some call it a 'gut' feeling, though I always remember a student attending one of my courses naming it for himself as a 'knowing' and that resonated with me. If you have learned to listen to your body then you will certainly know what I'm talking about. It's that feeling when everything in your body feels positive or negative, depending on the situation you find yourself in.

Another student of mine once revealed 'There's a new person at work who really winds me up and I don't know why but I really dislike her'.

We don't always have to know the reason, but our body never lies, whereas our mind constantly plays tricks on us. If you learn to listen to your body you will take the short cut to getting where you want to be, whereas if you listen to your head you may take all sorts of paths that don't 'feel' right and your body will probably suffer the consequences.

So many people suffer with all sorts of ailments and even serious health conditions simply because they didn't listen to the signals that were loud and clear. Many people have written books about this very subject, Louise Hay 'Heal Your Life' and David Hamilton 'How Your Mind Can Heal Your Body' to name but two who have had a great deal of influence on my thinking.

Here is an example of when my intuition worked for me . . . .

After deciding to change direction with my career I hit a very questioning time which resulted in me feeling I was on 'shaky ground'. I knew my energy was fired up when working on my spiritual growth, but as soon as I tried to direct my attention toward the bread and butter side of my business my energy changed and I had felt for some time that I was being pulled away from that part of it, but it felt irresponsible as I needed that part of my work to keep my earnings at a level to survive.

My ego was reacting big time as I began to look for another source of income. I had a chance to work as a nurse on a night shift in a residential home. It *felt* so wrong and when I was initially asked I was torn between listening to my intuition which said 'No, you don't need to do this, something else will come along, versus my left brain saying 'What are you thinking about, be responsible and get out there and just do it.' I hesitated and said I'd think about it and get back to them. I felt as if I would be stepping back in time, having previously run a small residential home for the elderly and lived in it with my family for seven years, followed by working as a Manager in a larger Residential home for another four years. Hence, I was finding it very uncomfortable to step back into those shoes again as previously it had led me to experience 'burn out' and I had purposefully stepped out of that role when my intuition led me to work as a personal development trainer.

I went and sat in the garden to think about it logically with my left brain dominating my thoughts. It did make sense to swallow hard and get on with it, so after a lot of debating between my thoughts and feelings I allowed my left brain to win and denied my right brain (intuitive side) to have a voice. However when I rang back to offer my services I was informed that the shift had been given to another nurse. I felt a great sense of relief. I had been taken care of! My right brain won after all—hooray! My body immediately lost its tension and felt free and I knew I would be looked after as a result . . . and I was. I was offered work in training from a source that was completely new to me and hence led to much bigger opportunities!

Another occasion when I tried to address my 'left' brains desire to sort out my finances, I set out for an interview to sell programmes at an annual event in the area. Again, it felt so wrong but my ego (left brain) was telling me to be sensible and do something to increase my income.

I decided to go along and find out more but on the way there I started to feel very emotional, until the tears were pouring down my face. How could I face an interview looking like this! However I was not allowing myself to get out of it that easily, so I drove on until I arrived at the gate. It was not very clear how to find the office and I felt at a loss as to where to go. Then I was aware of time passing and began to worry about being late. It began to dawn on me that I wasn't meant to go and decided to drive off, with an immense feeling of relief again!

My body knew far more than I dared to admit to but gradually I was becoming more and more aware of just how powerful my intuition was and more importantly how to listen to it. Remember—your body never lies!

Lessons can come in all shapes and sizes and we don't always learn the significance of them until later. However much I doubted and felt anxious I never stopped 'trusting' for a moment. To me that was what kept me going through all the 'shaky' moments.

I realized I had truly stepped onto my 'inner journey' when I started acting on my 'inner voice' without understanding why. And when exactly, you may ask did that happen . . .

Well I guess it really began many moons ago when I was a naive seventeen year old. Looking back I recognised how often synchronicities had played a part in my life; I just wasn't aware of them until later when I understood more about them. At College I made friends with a fellow student Jeni, who was lodging with a lady called Irene, who we later discovered was telepathic. We were both intrigued by her and would spend many hours having lengthy discussions about all sorts of issues around 'why people behave the way they do'. Irene seemed to know us so well and on occasions would say things to us which we had been thinking before we had a chance to open our mouths. As we grew away from that part of our lives neither of us were aware of just how much of an influence Irene had actually had on us individually.

When I was young I always wanted to teach but never considered myself clever enough to go to teachers training college so didn't even attempt it. I ended up going away to train as a nurse, even though I was very squeamish. How strange was it that many years later, I found myself training adults, or was it strange at all?!! For the first time in my life I 'felt' I was doing what *felt* right. That '*knowing*' feeling is so different from that feeling 'I will make the most of it', which so many of us experience when we are not doing what we really feel is right for us. Even though we may not know what we want to do we can identify the feeling when we're doing the wrong thing or find ourselves in the wrong relationship. Being in a relationship can be very difficult if we are not connected at a 'soul' level. A true connection is not about possession, it's about allowing your partner to be free, knowing that what you have and share together holds no boundaries and you are together where ever you are.

I have been very privileged in having many soul connections throughout my life and understand that I was meant to experience many different types of relationships in order to understand what relationships are about and to assist others to intuitively follow their own paths rather than be influenced by others. I do believe that we were all born with our own lessons to learn and if you look around you it is often quite obvious what people's lessons are. Some are tested with health issues all through their lives, others with finance or relationships. Of course most of us will have a combination of many lessons but some of us do seem to be particularly tested in one area and for me I would have to say it definitely feels as if it's been relationships.

My first love had a powerful affect on me and when it came to a sudden end I was devastated, even though I had anticipated that we may grow apart eventually, I just wasn't prepared for it when it happened. My first real taste of rejection and abandonment was a huge lesson and I learnt to duck and dive well to avoid repeating that lesson. However by doing so I created many other lessons which were just as painful and so my journey on relationships had begun . . . .

Each relationship has taught me many things, mostly about myself and sometimes I have unintentionally repeated the lesson with the next relationship. However, when I have recognized the lesson I have been able to move on quicker without experiencing the hurt all over again or as intensely.

One of my truly amazing relationships was with Robin. I met him when I was training to be a nurse. He was admitted into casualty and then onto accident ward, where I was working at the time. He was the driver in a fatal car crash. His fiancée and mother were with him and sadly his fiancée died and his mother was taken to intensive care with numerous injuries. Robin had a broken leg.

Over the following weeks I would spend time with Robin allowing him to talk his feelings out and was filled with sympathy for him. I chaperoned him to visit his mother who was still attached to a lot of tubes and even though Robin was a medical student he was very vulnerable when it came to seeing his own mother looking as poorly as she did. I tried to prepare him but he still looked shocked when confronted with her. Despite being full of guilt Robin never lost his wonderful sense of humour which seemed to support him through his darkest hours.

I left the ward before Robin left the hospital so said my goodbyes and wished him well.

After several months I received a letter addressed very formally to me as he did not even know my Christian name. Those were the days when we were formally addressed! His letter was one of thanks for all the support I gave him and he also asked me if I would allow him to treat me to dinner.

I was stunned and very touched. Of course I accepted and so a six month relationship commenced.

Robin opened my eyes to my own creativity. He encouraged me to write, a passion I had from childhood but had not pursued. We went on holiday to Derbyshire and walked for miles while staying at different B&B's and I became more aware of nature and simple pleasures in life that I had lost touch with previously. Robin was tender and caring and along with his gift to smile and laugh so readily I grew to love him very dearly.

However our relationship ended when our lives naturally took different paths. I don't even remember how or when exactly, so that indicates to me that we must have let go very willingly.

Robin returned to London to continue his training but although he had all the qualities to make an excellent Doctor he struggled with the politics and his real love was hockey.

It was no great surprise to me when I learned years later that Robin did complete his training, but eventually left medicine and went to pursue his dream of becoming a Hockey teacher. He listened and followed his intuition. I learnt so much from that man! He taught me to follow my intuition by writing more which in turn opened opportunities for me also.

Robin opened a door for me and showed me how to value myself and also how to get in touch with my creativity. I will always treasure the memories of him. I believe that everyone comes into our life for a reason even though we may not be able to work out what it is at the time.

TRUSTING MY INTUITION

'Time' My time is valuable so I will spend more doing things and being with people that fulfil me.

It was 1999 and I was at Gatwick airport waiting to go on holiday. I decided to go and choose a book that I could lose myself in. As I arrived at the book stand I was instantly drawn to a book that was being well publicised 'The Journey' by Brandon Bayes. I read the back cover and knew that was the book for me, so bought it. I'm usually quite a slow reader but on this occasion I was totally absorbed by Brandon's story that I could hardly put it down. However I knew her story was affecting me on a personal level and soon recognised that I was looking for change in my life and she was helping me to find it.

After finishing the book I knew I would be acting on what I read in some way, but had no idea how. Soon after reading that book another one came to my attention 'The Psychic Pathway' by Sonia Choquette. Again I was personally moved by the words and as I approached the end of the book I was thinking 'What could I do with all that I was feeling' Of course it was no coincidence that as I turned to the very end of the book I read 'If you want to run a course from Sonia's work, contact her.'

It was as if my question had been answered . . . . and that's how it works, ask and it is given! And as another saying goes: 'Be careful what you ask for'. In the years to follow I learnt so much about the power of my thoughts.

Once I began my journey on self discovery it became addictive as it so often does. I read more books, attended more workshops and was drawn more and more to working with others and helping them on their journey's too.

Having trained as a counsellor and previously a nurse I had been involved in the caring profession for many years already. This time it felt different though. I found myself exploring my childhood dreams of being a teacher, which I had never pursued before. Learning to listen to my intuition led me to train as a trainer which opened a whole new career for me. For the first time in my life I felt I was really doing something that *felt* right. As a nurse I so often struggled as I was squeamish but my need to please others, led me into a profession that didn't quite sit comfortably with me, though I felt I was doing it for a reason, of which I would discover later . . . .

So my journey as a personal development trainer had begun and hence I soon started running courses on 'Developing Intuition' and was amazed how individuals lives began to change, along with mine, as we listened more and more to that 'inner voice' we all have deep inside us. Understanding that we all have our own answers and learning to access it can be the most empowering thing for some people. As I unleashed my own inner voice my confidence and self esteem immediately blossomed. I have since watched many individuals be amazed at their own discoveries which have led them to the biggest revelation of all . . . learning to truly value themselves. This leads to questioning every relationship we have ever had and soon we can measure our self value by who we 'allow' into our lives. If you are surrounded by people who value you then your own self value is good but if you have a lot of 'needy' and 'demanding' people around you it may be time to look at your own 'value system'. We cannot change others behaviour toward us but we can certainly change our response to them, often resulting in a very different response back from them.

Sharon decided that she was fed up always taking the blame when she and her partner John had an argument. John would verbally attack her, knowing exactly how to hurt her.

As Sharon learnt to respond differently, John no longer felt gratification from his comments so ceased to continue with his derogative remarks.

When I was training as a counsellor I soon recognised my desire to work with groups. I remember so clearly sitting in the classroom listening to my tutor and thinking *'one day I'll be doing what you're doing'*. How significant it was when 7years later I was doing exactly what he was doing, as a tutor for adult education, delivering counselling courses and in the same room! The power of thought—I never doubt it anymore! Be careful what you wish for . . . .

Learning to listen and act on my intuition opened up a whole new way of living and I've never looked back.

It taught me so many valuable lessons, some of which included:

To value myself in a way I had never previously done.
Not take other peoples actions so personally.
To dare to take risks and accept the consequences.
To live life in the 'now'.
To be patient.
To accept what happens and learn from it.

Allowing life to unfold and not try to force the outcome, was probably one of the biggest lessons I received.

As a group leader I discovered the 'magic' in what makes an individual open up in front of complete strangers and actually start to move forward in their lives, when previously they have been unable to do so.

As soon as I ask a group to agree to a 'group contract' I sense a feeling of relief and safety enter the room. Even though they know there is no guarantee that everyone will keep it, it's as if they sense the importance of what they are committing to, not just for themselves but for others as well and an unspoken bond forms between them. I have even been reminded to repeat the contract rules if a new member has joined the group.

Within a very short time individuals feel safe to explore and reveal issues they have often kept hidden for years. It has certainly made me very aware of the lack of 'care' that exists in society as a whole. So many people are locked in their own grief and torment, never feeling 'safe enough' to share it and sadly they often feel this with their nearest and dearest, causing distance to grow between them, resulting in relationship break ups, when all that was necessary was a few golden rules which would have allowed them to explore issues that could have been worked through.

At times I have felt very humbled when working with clients who have made major steps forward even though their world was in chaos. With support, love and kindness we are able to make incredible steps in a direction we have never dared venture before. Patch Adams demonstrated this very well through his own journey and continues to bring love and laughter to those who have come in touch with his followers.

My own journey began to twist and turn and I became involved in training care staff in residential homes. An area I knew well and it was lovely to spend time with those who devoted their lives to caring for others, whilst not always being cared for themselves. I continued to emphasise the importance of looking after ourselves.

How can we truly be there for someone else if we have not looked after ourselves first? Many find this difficult as they have been so used to putting everyone before them. However I learnt this lesson well when running my own Residential Home while bringing up a family. Living in meant 24hrs commitment and it wasn't too long before I recognised the meaning of 'burn out'.

It wasn't until it was pointed out to me that I needed to support myself better if I was to continue with such a big commitment, that I took some action. By allowing myself time and activities that fulfilled me I was able to give from my heart once again and everyone gained around me. Being allowed to address my own needs resulted in me being a happier person, therefore more focused and relaxed when I was working with others and also more able to be the sort of mother I wanted to be.

I urge mothers everywhere to examine your own needs and not try to ignore them as you are role models to your children. We teach more by example than anything else and if our children see that we don't allow ourselves pleasures then they will grow up feeling that is what is expected of them. Our children will grow into healthy adults if we just provide a simple ingredient—LOVE. Material possessions will never replace what we give from our hearts. You only have to talk to adults who have been deprived of this one ingredient and it is obvious how starved they felt and often still feel the same way well into adulthood.

I have learnt that in order to give love we must learn what love feels like first . . . .

Many clients I have worked with have had to revisit their 'loveless' childhood and work through their own grief and it can be very painful. For those brave enough to venture there, the results can be dramatic.

My interest in this work led me to train as a Regression therapist and again I have witnessed many clients clearing blocks that have held them back for years.

Since starting my own journey with intuition I have been constantly amazed at how my life has flowed more easily, even though I'm often challenged in ways I would previously not known how to deal with. The difference is I now don't have the need to have all the answers immediately and instead trust they will come when they are needed. That doesn't mean I'm never uncomfortable, of course at times I am, but I know deep inside I will be looked after if I don't panic. I recognise that I'm just learning another lesson and try to recognise what it is instead of pushing it to one side and ignoring it as I used to.

A JOURNEY OF INTUITION IN NEW ZEALAND

**with a guide and opportunity to record
your own lessons . . . .**

*'Attention' I will give my focal attention
to every new situation I encounter.*

I had reached what some would describe as the 'delicate age' of fifty years and to rejoice it, I had booked a trip to New Zealand for five weeks. Now, sitting at Heathrow airport eager to experience whatever the universe had planned for me, I reflected on when my journey really began . . .

My awareness was alerted when I asked for help from a source I wasn't even sure existed and then decided to listen to the voice deep inside me and realised it was talking and responding to me. This excited me and I wanted more, who wouldn't, it was like a drug and I was becoming addicted to the exhilaration I experienced when I indulged in it. I explored, I read, I prayed, but most of all I saw results . . . then came conflict. It became very evident that I couldn't do all these exciting things without it affecting my world that I had known for so long. Change was becoming apparent in me and naturally it was affecting those close to me, resulting in uncomfortable feelings for both them and myself. Gradually I was aware that I couldn't deny the growth that was taking place within me, but at the same time there was a price to pay. It was hard and I denied the choices I knew I would have to make, for as long as possible.

Conflict lead to unrest and because I was learning to listen to my 'inner voice' so much more I couldn't deny what was loud and clear because DESIRE was growing stronger and stronger. I just couldn't fit back into the world I had known. The discovery I had made was too good to turn my back on and more than that—it was the TRUTH—all around and about me. Suddenly I felt I was living in truth and it was time to stand up for what I believed. I prayed for help and direction and was blessed with tools to lead me forward, which continued to come as my journey progressed.

Learning to develop my intuition was the key to my happiness as negative events changed into 'challenging lessons'. My whole outlook on life was growing more positive as I learned to accept others for what they were and detach my personal feelings from how they behaved toward me. My journey became an adventure and I allowed myself to explore avenues that I had never ventured down before. Dreams became more meaningful . . . especially one, where I found myself wanting to jump out of an aeroplane, but frozen with fear . . . a warm, strong voice from behind whispered 'TRUST' and I did and flew through the clouds, knowing that I was completely being looked after. That voice, I learned was my 'inner voice' and gradually I listened to it more and more.

As I explored New Zealand on the internet trying to get some sense of where to begin my journey I contacted some likeminded souls over there. Wendy, a woman who seemed to welcome travellers into her home contacted me and we corresponded by email and as my trip drew nearer she suggested I start my adventure with her. I was so grateful to her for this offer and even more so when she offered a friend to meet me at the airport. What a gentle start that would be. She lived in Raglan, near

Hamilton on the North Island. That was perfect as I was landing in Auckland, a comfortable travelling distance away. So here I was at Heathrow airport ready to experience whatever the universe was about to offer me!

As I prepared for the trip of a lifetime I slowly became aware of just how much my comfort zones were going to be stretched. Never had I ventured so far or for so long on my own, with no one familiar to support me when I may feel vulnerable, sort me out when I get in a muddle, listen to me when I need to talk. No one there just when I may need them most!

Of course you could say living on my own should have prepared me for all of that, but it's not the same as I always had the telephone should I experience loneliness or vulnerability and knowing that friends and family were always nearby was a constant comfort in itself, even if I didn't actually act upon it.

As I packed my case, prepared my paperwork, I wondered what my trip would bring, who would I meet, what would I see, why am I even going there and what will I bring back with me in the way of personal growth? I had felt something calling me to New Zealand for quite a while but had no idea what or why, but I was sure I was going to find out. I also sensed that I was meant to go alone, as I nearly went with a friend, but it was not to be and relationships seemed to have distanced from my life just at a time when I was going away. I believed I was meant to be absolutely free at this time so that I had no distractions pulling me back or distracting my energy.

So many questions unanswered and so impatient to find the answers but I knew everything was just as it should be and all would be revealed when it was meant to be. All I had to do was allow myself to be lead by my intuition, as I so passionately believed that part of me always knows best.

I prepared myself for a journey of '*intuition*'. I promised myself that every step of the way I would allow myself to act completely on my intuition and from here on my journal will record every experience as a lesson and what I learnt from it and I hope by reading this some of you may discover your own 'inner voice' and learn to trust it enough to act on it as I did and still do.

Mon 31ˢᵗ Jan 05

The day had finally arrived . . . after planning; visualising and talking to numerous people about it . . . I am actually about to experience five weeks in New Zealand, travelling alone. It's going to be a 'huge' experience for me as I've never even been on holiday abroad alone, but right from the seed of thought I was driven to do just this—why? I have no idea, as yet of course, but it feels so right and although I step forward with trepidation I know I'm going to be so looked after by the universe, amongst tests I have no doubt I will have to endure along the way . . . .

I woke at 6am to a beautiful moon shining directly into my bedroom. It felt like a sign saying 'we're here, and will be with you every step of the way.' After having spent an evening debating on what to put in my suitcase and what to leave behind, I finally decided to take the laptop as hand luggage, as I've been well and truly tested on learning how to use it!! Having decided, I realised that it would be useful in writing up my journal and I now feel perhaps I should keep it with me to ensure it's as safe as possible.

By 9.30am I was saying goodbye to No 24, my precious space and prayed I would return safely to be welcomed home on 8ᵗʰ March.

My dear, trusted friend Linda and biggest fan of all my work was ready to receive me and my luggage so we may commence our journey to Heathrow. I was so appreciative of her giving up her precious time, not only to chauffeur me to the airport but also to collect me at the end of my travels. I have no doubt that I will welcome seeing her there at the end of my journey.

So far, so good, we arrived in good time and had lunch while waiting to check in and then came . . .

LETTING GO

I suddenly discovered my water bottle had leaked in my bag and had spilled all over my mobile phone. I tried to dry it with a hand dryer and even searched for a mobile phone shop and asked if they could do anything, but no joy!! I guess I shall just have to wait and see what happens if not invest in a cheap phone in NZ and make the most of it. I believed totally in synchronicities so there had to be a reason why this happened! Of course 'letting go' isn't just about walking away with all the safe connections in place. It's about truly 'letting go' and really allowing myself to 'feel' vulnerable. Losing attachment of my mobile phone certainly put me in touch with a sense of 'loss' and even 'panic'. However I sensed deep inside that I would be looked after, so was able to move forward and walk away from my one attachment left, Linda.

When I arrived at the departure gate it was time to say goodbye— now the rest of my journey would be alone, or would it?!! Who knows what the universe has in store? With that thought came a mixture of excitement, anticipation and of course fear!

Once I boarded the plane, everything seemed to be going according to schedule. I found my aisle seat, as requested and then soon after one of the hostesses or rather host, asked if I'd like to have more room. I realised it was because the couple next to me had asked for more space and it would be easier if I was the one to move. It was not a problem and I ended up sitting next to a lovely older lady, Moira, who was also travelling alone and we had a spare seat between us which meant we could spread our belongings more comfortably. She had lived in NZ for 20 years and was going back to visit her daughter. Moira now worked as a 'carer' on nights in a nursing home in Nottingham, where she now lived. A profession I knew well and had been connected with for years. I had run a small Residential Home for the elderly for some years and worked as a Manager in two other homes, so it felt 'meant' that we were to sit together for this long haul and I felt comforted by the similarity of our lives.

We connected immediately and I was so glad I had been asked if I would move seats. Her daughter owned a travel agent on the south island, near Queenstown. I wonder if I'll meet up with her again?!!

How does **Lesson 1 'Letting Go'** relate to you in your life . . . .

This is such an important lesson and a good starting point, as I learnt at the very beginning of my trip. Without letting go of some of my home comforts I couldn't be open to allow new experiences in.

In order to move forward you may need to explore what you are holding on to. Maybe a relationship that is causing you grief, or a home that you don't feel comfortable in, or maybe a job that is distressing you, or even a friendship that is one sided?

Be honest with yourself and even if you are not ready to change at least recognise what may need to change. Remember, the first step to changing anything is admitting to yourself that it needs changing. Then you can take small steps towards achieving it.

For instance, if you know your job is no longer serving you and a good sign to recognise this would be if you wake up in the morning filled with dread at the prospect of facing another day doing it, then start the process of change by first exploring alternative possibilities. Perhaps scan the job section in the newspaper and become aware of how your body responds when you read the different adverts. Recognise when your body is telling you 'that's a job I'd like' or 'I could imagine doing that'. Then spend some time imagining yourself in a new job and let your imagination expand and develop so the dream draws nearer and you can really feel how different your life could be if you were doing this new job. As we free ourselves of old patterns, we invite new energies in and life will never be the same again. Of course that in itself brings challenging lessons and we need to be ready for them. Fear of change often holds us back from doing the one thing we desire, so we may need to explore why we resist change before we decide to blame outside forces, which is so much easier.

Once you have explored 'why' you do not welcome change and you may need assistance with this as it's very difficult to look objectively at your own issues, then you can move more freely to inviting change into your life. Often our resistance to change is very deep rooted so you may well discover some truths about yourself which for years you have not realised were there. Be gentle with yourself and allow the process of accepting *why you don't like change* to work before moving onto actualising change. It always amazes me how once we know the 'why's' we naturally move more easily into the next stage of 'allowing' it to happen. It's rather like an ill person who doesn't know what's wrong with them. Once a diagnosis is made, however negative it may be, the person generally moves forward even with grief, as now they know what they are dealing with. As humans we have a natural need to 'know' and once addressed it stops us generating fear, from worrying about the unknown. To lose someone because they have gone missing is a grief unresolved, so the person can never reach a stage of acceptance, an intolerable place to be as they are forever waiting in hope, making it is very difficult to move forward . . .

Carl Rogers, the person centred psychologist always believed that we have a natural tendency to reach our full potential whatever the circumstances, so when we are held in a place of 'out of control' our growth becomes stunted and eventually it will affect us in other ways. As our minds and bodies are so connected in every way we will gradually feel the effects both emotionally and physically.

It is for this reason that I believe the cognitive approach of changing our thought patterns can be very useful but only long term if the reasons for the 'faulty' thinking are addressed too. To change anything about us without understanding the causes is to me like putting the sticky plaster on without bothering to clean the wound first. The holistic approach of attending to the 'whole' person may take longer but it will most likely last longer as well.

*I invite you to explore **lesson 1** . . . .*

Record your experiences of 'letting go' or 'not letting go when you would have liked to have done'

Is there anything/anyone you would like to let go of now.

_____

_____

_____

_____

_____

_____

_____

_____

_____

_____

Tues. 1st Feb 05

A very comfortable, smooth flight enhanced by nurturing airline staff. I took the Australian bush flower remedy 'Travel' religiously throughout the journey, as recommended by Wendy, from New Zealand, and so far I can tell it seems to have worked well as I feel amazingly refreshed, considering I had very little sleep. Mobile telephone still inactive!!

Twelve hours later once off the flight at Singapore I lost contact with Moira and went for a walkabout and fortunately found the hotel a friend from home had told me about where I could get a shower for $8. Perfect and I went one better and treated myself to a manicure as well!

A good start to my hols and my nails had been looking in a bad state so it was a bonus to get them back into shape. It didn't seem too long before we were boarding again for the next long haul to Auckland . . . New Zealand here I come!!

I'm getting totally confused about the time as Singapore is 8hrs ahead of U.K. and now I'm about to go to a country which is 5 more hours ahead—so 13hrs ahead of U.K altogether. At the moment I shall just go with the flow and keep taking the flower remedy!

I can't believe I threw my boarding ticket in the bin with my rubbish before lining up to board! Panic crept over me as I rummaged after it and luckily retrieved it as no one had put anything in after me. No surprise when there were a few raised eyebrows as I rejoined the queue!

On this flight I was seated beside a very friendly older couple from, guess where, NORFOLK! I felt comforted to be joined by folk from home, which added to the very pleasant smooth flight where once again I was looked after by excellent Singapore airline staff . . . but more dramas were about to present themselves before I was to meet Wendy!

LESSON 2

PAY ATTENTION

When going through customs, security decided to check my hand luggage where my laptop was packed, though fortunately they didn't want me to get it out. While scanning the bag they spotted an apple that I had bought at Singapore airport. They questioned me and it didn't help that I had ticked (by mistake) that I was declaring food into the country! So I was taken away for questioning and finally fined $200. What an expensive apple!! As I wrote out the cheque the security man said 'I do hope this doesn't put you off our country'

'Well, it's not a very good start, is it?' I smiled weakly.

The couple I had met on the plane stayed back to check that I was ok, which I really appreciated. I was determined not to let this ruin the start of my holiday, though have to admit I did once again feel very vulnerable.

It felt like a 'wake up' call, telling me to 'Be alert, you cannot rely on anyone else to look out for you.' Too many times in my life I've relied too heavily on others and consequently they have either let me down, or I've discovered that I've actually known best, but not believed in myself enough to trust my own judgement.

Finally through customs I couldn't find a lady holding a banner with my name on it as arranged by Wendy, so I phoned Wendy, having now bought a phone card as my mobile still hadn't come back to life. Trish had also phoned Wendy, concerned that I hadn't appeared with everyone else so had gone to sit down with the banner on her lap. Eventually we found each other and I was so relieved not to be stranded on the other side of the world. Trish, who came from South Africa though born in Rhodesia, was very friendly and welcoming. About my age with short blonde wavy hair and warm sensitive eyes I sensed immediately I would get along with her. I so appreciated her making time to come and meet me when she knew nothing about me and had no reason to do it other than because Wendy had asked her. I soon learned that this was natural behaviour in New Zealand where travellers were given a lot of care and attention.

We set out for another journey to Wendy's after Trish kindly stopped at her sisters to borrow her nephews spare mobile for me to use while on holiday, as my battery and SIM card were still working. A problem so simply resolved!

We finally arrived at Wendy's in Raglan and she welcomed me with open arms. As the day wore on I met others who were staying with her as well. Later I went to the beach with Bill, one of Wendy's houseguests, a traveller from California and saw Trish again with Bronwin, another friend of Wendy's. I didn't feel like going in the water just yet as I was very weary and wanted to get used to the sun gradually. The weather was glorious, about 21c with light showers periodically. Wendy's home was in a beautiful setting with an equally beautiful view of mountains, hilltops with a variety of different types of dwellings all radiating an energy of their own.

How does **Lesson 2 'Pay Attention'** *relate to us in our life* . . . .

My 2nd lesson was a real shock as I had no idea that I had done anything wrong by having an apple in my hand luggage. It would be very easy to blame that on the fact that I was over tired from all the hours of travelling, or that I didn't hear or see anything that notified me of the 'no fresh food into NZ' law. However, the truth was, I was not paying attention and I needed to, especially as I was now in a foreign country where the rules may be different to the ones I was familiar to back home.

Do you pay enough attention? How much do you miss, by not being attentive? I don't mean just paying attention to the obvious but also to the things that are not so obvious. How often do you really pay attention to the signals that your body gives you. Remember our bodies never lie; it is only our minds that play tricks. When we are faced with a difficult person or situation, our body gives us messages on how we really feel. If we chose to ignore the signals that our bodies give us, eventually, if we are continuously exposed to these same people or situations the signals will get louder until in the end 'If you don't sort it, it sorts you.' This often comes in the form of an illness or an accident, so you are then forced to stop and take stock.

Pay attention and *get out of your own way*, before you trip yourself up. You can be sure if you don't take this lesson seriously you will know all about it, just as I did!

I invite you to explore **lesson 2** . . . .

Take time to really pay attention in a way you don't usually and then record what you noticed when you did.

Pay attention to your body's signals and record what you felt it was telling you.

_____

_____

_____

_____

_____

_____

_____

_____

Thurs. 3rd Feb 05 8.45am

Whatever happened to Wednesday 2nd?!! I'm sitting on a veranda outside my bedroom (or rather Wendy's bedroom that she so kindly gave up for me). I can hear Cicada's filling the air with their chatter and they remind me of crickets. It's a glorious day and the temperature is comfortably hot, though no sun at present. I woke about 7am and felt so much better for a good nights sleep. I had finally retired at 9pm after sharing a supper with Wendy, Alexa and Ben, surf academy students, Bronwin, Ben's Mother and Bill. I did feel overwhelmed after all my travelling, trying so hard to engage in all the conversations going on around me and at the same time trying to remember who everyone was. My journey had begun to catch up on me, despite overdosing on the Bach flower remedy 'Travel', which I certainly think helped.

Today would be about finding my feet and hopefully my head again and then maybe sorting out transport and getting e-mails out, at least that's the plan anyway!

After enjoying a relaxed breakfast, Wendy drove me to Hamilton, the nearest town, after calling on Andy, a friend of hers who lived nearby, to see if he could get my laptop to connect with the Internet. Unfortunately, no joy so we'll have to visit a computer shop later.

Once in town we meandered around the shops and had a spot of lunch. At last Wendy and I had time alone, when we had a chance to connect more. I'm beginning to feel more settled and less concerned even though I haven't solved the problem I had this morning (the internet connection) but somehow it seemed to be in a better proportion now! I felt absorbed by Wendy's lovely energy as she shared some of her life with me.

It seemed as if she had devoted much of it helping others and obviously loved having her home used as a stop gap for travellers as well as looking after students in their time of need. After lunch we both had a successful buy, me a loose shirt for the days I may need to cover up and Wendy bought a lovely colourful top that really suited her.

I also invested in a new lead for the computer in hope that it will solve the laptop problems. We called into the car hire shop and I booked a hire car for the duration of my stay, which I will collect tomorrow . . . things are taking shape thanks to Wendy's guidance.

I bought a few things from the supermarket and Wendy bought a huge basketful of food to cater for her lodgers. It took me back to the days of catering for eight plus people, when I ran and lived in my residential home for three elderly people plus husband, daughter and two step children and even lodgers who came and went. It feels as though that was another lifetime, as my life is so different now and I am feeling empowered by the freedom of living alone.

Tonight Wendy and I sat talking, drinking wine and eating incredible blue cheese till 1am and it felt as if I'd known her for ages. Two spiritual beings from opposite ends of the world come together to connect and share their own individual journeys that have brought them to this point. How special it felt and how privileged I felt to be experiencing it. Wendy has a compassion for the human race entwined with an almost teenage like humour. She really is stimulating to be with and yet at the same time calming.......what a beautiful combination!

Fri 4ᵗʰ Feb 05

Today I managed to connect to the Internet after more hours of frustration and changing to a NZ server. Andy, Wendy's friend has been very generous with his time and I'm so grateful, but not enough to have sex with him as Wendy thought perhaps I should?!!

Bill is good company too and the three of us enjoyed a supper of muscles, salad, potato and wine. Wayne (Wendy's platonic friend!) decided to drop by, as everyone seems to in Wendy's house! Again so similar to the life I used to know. It feels so strange not to lock up when we go out, in fact I feel quite nervous about leaving valuables around but I was assured that I don't need to worry as no one does here, so I guess I'm being tested on 'trust' again! It really is like going back in time in England, when we also didn't feel the need to be quite so paranoid about security issues.

I've noticed over the last two days how we're all becoming so much more relaxed in each other's company and our true colours are beginning to show!

LESSON 3

BELIEVE IN YOURSELF

I felt very tested by Wendy today . . . when driving back from Hamilton I was following her in my 'gold automatic Nissan' hired car when she decided to put her foot down and overtook two cars leaving me to find my own way! Suddenly I felt so vulnerable and realised I needed to have more faith in myself and not rely totally on Wendy. I had been calmly following her with no great concern or even interest in where I was actually going. I knew I could find my own way back if I trusted my instinct. Thankfully I saw the road sign to Wendy's and turned and there she was, waiting further up, grinning like a Cheshire cat! I didn't know whether to be angry or thankful! I settled for being just grateful that I wasn't actually lost!

I was aware of how little confidence I had in myself and it wasn't until it was tested that I appreciated my own ability.

*How does **Lesson 3 'Believe in Yourself'** relate to us in our life . . . .*

This is another tough one as we are so often our own worst critic! Being in New Zealand I should have realised that I was more than capable of looking after myself but it was so much easier to just 'follow' rather than think for myself. How often have we allowed another to lead us or convince us of something when deep inside we want to question it? A lack of confidence or belief in our self can so easily result in us being too influenced by an outsider. If we truly want to live a life where we will feel fulfilled we have to learn to listen and believe in ourself first. How can we learn to do that? Once again, baby steps give the best results . . . .

*I invite you to explore **lesson 3** . . . .*

Explore when you have followed another's advice and wish you hadn't. If you could turn the clock back what would you have done instead. Was it a lack of trust in your own judgement that lead you to follow another's advice? If yes, assess where your judgement is now.

Keep a journal—this will increase your development and heighten your awareness and if possible join a group where you can develop your intuition together. You will learn from sharing each other's experiences. It's a fun subject to explore and the more you lighten up and allow it to happen the more you will discover your own intuition.

Sat 5th Feb 05

Today was 'Sound Splash' a reggae festival at Raglan, near the beach. I ventured down with Bill at 9.30am to see the 'Dolphin Dance' performed by Maori girls dressed in beautiful turquoise, blue and green dresses. They wore face paint and even silver paint in their hair. I noticed a lot of the men wore dreadlocks, and was told by Kayla that it's quite a usual sight here in New Zealand. The dolphin dance was in aid of saving the dolphins from being tagged, as it's very stressful for them, which then causes many to abort their young. Having swum with these beautiful creatures a year ago in Cuba with my dear friend Dulce I felt 100% behind their cause and felt quite moved watching them demonstrate so perfectly the emotions of the dolphins. Their bright costumes and exaggerated makeup merely emphasised their emotions even more. I felt tears well up in my eyes as their bodies demonstrated the dolphin's plight and I watched in total empathy.

Kayla and I went back to Raglan, leaving Bill to mingle with the crowd and for the first time I ventured around the local area that I was staying in. It was small, with quaint, interesting shops and eating-places. I had coffee with Kayla and sampled for the first time a chi tea, which I agreed was very tasty. Kayla dropped me back at Wendy's to chill for a few hours before going back to the festival when it would be in full swing. The house was empty and it felt really good to have some space. I really hadn't had any time to myself since I arrived, so I caught up on my correspondence, sending e-mails. It did feel good to have access to communication with home again.

Kayla, her daughter and I went back to the festival at 4pm and by now the roads were heavy with traffic. Over 3,000 attended the event and there were bands playing continuously throughout the day into the night. Kayla and I indulged in Veggie curry and I couldn't resist a portion of some 'yummy' carrot cake, it was delicious! During the afternoon Kayla and I ventured down to the beach where once again I was in awe of this wonderful country with its amazing scenery, where we could so comfortably walk undisturbed by other like-minded people. If only I could bottle it and take it home to open and absorb on a grey, rainy day.

The music of the festival echoed across the land for miles and it felt surreal to be standing amongst it all and yet aware that I was on the other side of the world alone and feeling safe.

We finally left the festival after midnight, totally fed with reggae music, atmosphere and food and well and truly ready for bed.

Sun 6ᵗʰ Feb 05

I decided I needed a relaxing day after last night, so indulged in a lie in. When I eventually admitted to the day, I accompanied Bill to Raglan to collect my car as I had left it there the previous night having come back with Kayla rather than try and find it in the dark. Bill and I had a drink and shared part of our lives. Would you believe I've met another man with a catholic background! It seems to be a repeated lesson of mine and once again, it seemed to have affected his whole life, though this man is now firmly on his spiritual quest, unlike some I've met in the past.

Raglan is a dear little place and seems to attract backpackers, partly because it's renowned for attracting surfers. Bill showed me the local Back Packers Lodge and I was very impressed at just how clean and comfortable it was. I know they are not all alike, but I was told that back-packing in NZ is often better than expected, so I will certainly look out for them as they are so cheap, averaging out at $8 a night.

Later in the afternoon Kayla, Bill and I went to 'Bridal Veil Falls' in Waireinga, not far from Raglan. It was beautiful and the waterfall was 500m. Bill and Kayla went in for a swim but I was happy to sit and observe. We met another young couple that were visiting New Zealand for the first time as well, one from Canada and the other from New York.

Kayla told us to look through the waterfall at the rock behind for a short while and then look at the rock beside the fall and see what happens . . . the rock looked as though it was moving upwards—amazing!!

There were many steps to climb back up, but we slowly made it and walking through the bush, I was once again continuously distracted by the beautiful scenery around me.

Mon 7th Feb 05

Today proved to be another challenge—this time physical!

Bill and I set off to climb Mount Karoi, which is 756m high. We parked my car one side and drove to the other where we left Bill's car, which meant we could climb up one side and come down the other and have transport waiting, which we would probably be thankful for by then! It was very steep but I managed to keep up well with Bill, who was obviously very fit! The climb was through the bush and fortunately it was not too hot or sunny. It started to rain softly which was refreshing and the more I climbed the more I felt connected with the earth. Sometimes when we paused for a rest a small bird would hover above us. It seemed so tame and I felt it wanted to perch on my hand, yet not quite sure, perhaps it sensed I was a foreigner visiting its land! We had a picnic at the top with fruit/rice bread, bananas, nuts and water. My hands became cold and tingly and then numb so I put my jacket on and as we started our descend I knew it was going to be harder than going up as I was very conscious of blisters on my heel and my right knee was beginning to struggle, but I kept going, not that I had much choice at that point!

LESSON 4

TRUST YOUR INNER VOICE

I suddenly became aware that Bill had run on ahead and as I felt achy and tired I didn't feel very safe. Every corner I turned he was nowhere in sight and once again my vulnerability surfaced. The arrows were showing me the way, so I knew I didn't really need to worry, as I wasn't alone. However my knees were really hurting with every step and I was nervous of slipping and descending faster than intended! As I trusted and started to relax into the experience I eventually caught up with Bill, only to find him sitting on the grass waiting for me, looking quietly amused as I appeared some time later. My emotions were being tested by this man, but because I didn't know him very well I resisted telling, holding on to the little dignity I had left.

So we continued on what felt like a very spiritual journey through the bush, surrounded by an incredible quietness and misty rain which moistened the ground and trees around us. At times it felt as if we should whisper so as not to disturb the stillness that engulfed us. The view was magnificent and I was so grateful it wasn't hot and sunny, as I'm sure I wouldn't have had the stamina to cope with that as well.

As I reclaimed my car I followed Bill around the treacherous gravel tracks not knowing where we were going, but he went faster than I was comfortable with but I tried hard to keep up. Without any warning my car skidded right across the track and began to climb sideways up the embankment. I thought 'this is surely it!' Amazingly though it came back down and carried on as if it had never happened. I wanted to stop and gather myself but felt the need to find Bill as I was unsure where I was so continued to drive, though with more care than before. Bill was totally unaware of what had happened until I told him later back at Wendy's.

When I thought quietly about the incident I realised I didn't trust my own judgement enough and allowed myself to be led by another who had a complete understanding of driving on those sort of roads. I needed to stop allowing myself to be lead by others and trust my known instinct more. A harsh lesson, but one I needed to take on board before it returns to test me yet again!!

How does **Lesson 4** *relate to us in our life . . . .*

My inner voice was loud and clear but I still chose to ignore it as my left brain still had a big influence over me. Once again here I was in a vulnerable place, this time on a mountain with a man I hardly knew. I was feeling a great need to hold onto any security that presented itself, which on this occasion was Bill guiding me up and down a mountain. However, when he, like Wendy, left me unexpectedly alone, panic immediately set in which meant I lost all contact with my intuition. It actually took a near accident for me to 'wake up' to my inner voice.

Our 'inner' voice talks to us all the time. Whether we chose to listen to it or not depends a lot on the last lesson 'Believe in Yourself'. If we have not worked on that lesson first we have little chance of even hearing our 'inner' voice.

I invite you to explore **lesson 4** *. . . .*

Ask and record when you have heard your 'inner voice' and then when you have acted on it. Don't expect to run before you can walk, learn one lesson at a time. You will have fun learning these lessons and gradually your life will take a completely new meaning.

_____

_____

_____

LESSON 5

COMMUNICATE

We stopped to get some Thai food—unfortunately offending Wendy in the process as she was going to prepare us some food, unbeknown to us. I knew something was wrong by her energy and finally after confronting her with it, she talked about it and explained that in NZ there is a huge importance placed on serving food for guests. Neither of us appreciated that as we both came from countries that did not necessarily share the same values, or maybe not to the same extent as here.

As I had once housed lodgers and not been responsible for their meals, I certainly did not expect to be catered for by Wendy and neither did Bill but I found it interesting that even though we appear to speak the same language communication can be a problem! After the three of us voiced our feelings we progressed with our friendships.

*How can **Lesson 5** relate to us in our life . . . .*

Communication—boy, I could write a book on this one alone! Without good communication relationships break down and we constantly see evidence of this. Learning this lesson in NZ I recognised how easy it is to misinterpret what another may mean, especially when amongst people from another culture and I realised how easy it is when by meaning to get it right I actually got it so wrong. I guess I shouldn't have assumed I knew what Wendy would have liked Bill and me to do when returning from our mountain climb. I certainly didn't take on board that New Zealanders placed such an importance on feeding their house guests. I viewed myself as lodging at Wendy's as did Bill especially as I related to when I accommodated lodgers and had been used to them being independent and did not get involved with their meals. However Wendy didn't see Bill or me in that way and felt insulted when we brought a take away back. My huge lesson here is don't assume and acknowledge that everyone has their own way of doing things and it may be very different to mine. If we had communicated better we would never had to have had the difficult conversation that we had. However at least we did talk it through so good communication can also correct or mend wrong doings, whether meant intentionally or not.

Communication comes in many forms so be careful to be congruent with your body language as well as your speech. There is no point giving lip service if your body is screaming out opposite signals. I believe truth is the only way to live your life holistically. When we are in tune with our body and minds we live in harmony, but when we are trying to please and compromise at some stage the cracks will appear and trust will be lost. Although it can be very difficult to be totally honest and may cause hurt, there are ways of delivering it. If we 'own' our feelings instead of using accusations we are far more likely to open the channels of communication and move the relationship forward in a positive direction.

It is worth working on this lesson as it is the key to positive relationships.

ANITA MARTIN

*I invite you to explore **lesson 5** . . . .*

How do you view your communication skills? Take time to observe good and bad communication in others and record your findings. Then assess your own communication skills and record how you feel you are in the following areas: Do you really listen properly? Is your body language congruent with your words? Do you take time to fully understand what others mean and not jump to conclusions? Do others often want to talk to you about personal issues? Do you remember details that others tell you?

Record your findings and work on any areas that you feel need improving.

_____

_____

_____

_____

_____

_____

_____

_____

_____

Tues 8th Feb 05

Time to move on . . . after sorting and shopping I packed up, said my goodbyes to Wendy and Bill before going to Raglan to do some shopping. When I came to collect my bags the house was empty. I left a basket of fruit with a card and chocolate for Wendy and then took to the road—heading toward the Coromandel to my next destination which was to be Mana Retreat. It was about a 3hr journey and the views were so spectacular that I had to keep pulling in at lay-bys to absorb and catch them on camera what I never wanted to forget. Other travellers obviously had the same thoughts as we were continuously meeting along the road, cameras poised in hands with comments of 'Wow' 'Awesome' and other expressions of amazement as if we had just had a spiritual awakening, perhaps we had!

When I arrived I again became instantly aware of the beauty that surrounded me which had an amazing spiritual presence. The entrance up to the retreat was a long dark, almost eerie driveway which seemed to go on forever and at one point I wondered where it was leading to only to discover that I gone too far when I arrived at a private dwelling. Once there I needed a few moments to gather myself. This place was truly 'awesome' (a favourite word of the kiwis and fast becoming mine!) and had an ego of its own as it stood superior to miles of mountains, bush and lakes. It was engulfed in what felt like a healing energy and it was impossible not to be affected by it. Every pore of my body was soaking up the atmosphere.

Once I had made contact with the reception I was shown to my room, a beautifully kept wooden cabin with a double bed, en suite shower and even a desk and chair, perfectly positioned for writing my journal. At last I had found my own space, which I was so ready for after my busy week at Wendy's.

The whole centre was designed for peace and harmony and as it so rightly advertised to just 'Be'. Amara, who managed the centre, welcomed me like a friend and I soon met several other new visitors, who were also passing through. Catherine, from Denver and Amy who were sharing a campervan and Chantelle, a 32yr old who had come for a retreat, needing an escape from her high pressured job in London. There were several 'woofers' who I learned were backpackers who were working 6hr days to earn their keep. What a wonderful way to experience this beautiful country. They practically ran the place doing anything from picking organic vegetables and fruit, cooking meals and other domestic chores. What a fabulous place to work! Some would stay for months at a time—I wonder why?!!! The food was totally organic and always freshly picked and we were allowed unlimited quantities. I certainly did not feel guilty indulging in this type of food, as it radiated healthy living.

I had arrived at a perfect time, as there were no courses running, so meal times were very relaxed with no great time pressures. When I asked what time breakfast would be I was told 'It starts from 6.30am' . . . . big pause—and by now I'm panicking thinking I'll never be up for that—then he continued 'til about 10 and after that, it just means you help yourself.' Great, I thought, I'm definitely going to like it here. In fact I had to ask myself 'Will I need to move on?

To inform us of meal times a big gong would echo across the mountain, it felt a bit like being in a monastery (or nunnery in my case!!).

Wed 9th Feb 05

I woke naturally about 8.30am, which felt so good. I was rested and knowing I didn't have to rush had a leisure shower and ambled over to breakfast at about 9.30am. I filled myself up on fresh fruit salad (which had every fruit you could imagine) and yoghurt. After enjoying the company of other travellers I walked back to my precious space and spent the morning writing. It was so good not to have anyone else to consider, just me!

I had a long chat with Amara and she shared part of her life with me saying how she had given her notice in at Mana because it 'felt right' but she had no idea of what she would do next. I so related to that tale as I did the same thing nearly five years ago when I had been working as a Manager in a Residential Home. I decided to give my notice in knowing I had no other job in the offering. I had previously spent 7years running my own Residential Home and when my dear residents died I decided it was time for a change. However I fell into the trap so many of us do, of returning to work in an area where all my experience had been. So after another four years of repeating the work I had known so well albeit this time with added responsibility of staff and many more residents, I decided to REALLY listen to the universe. Boy did that change my life!

For a number of months I struggled to find enough work on a self employed basis, but was determined to pursue my dream of working as an independent trainer. I had felt that my life was standing still and I was so BORED!! After leaving my job I decided I must now do something that I really want. I had trained as a Counsellor, which had been an enormous journey in personal development, but so far had not used that qualification.

I spent time thinking about where my real desires lay and remembered someone once saying to me: 'If you don't know what to do, think back to your childhood and what you used to enjoy doing'. As children we live so much more in the moment and are honest with our desires. I remembered very clearly how much I enjoyed writing and always wanted to teach and used to pretend I was a teacher with an imaginary class. I had been a natural organiser and was often creating plays/concerts together with friends. Then I remembered when I reached my twenties I had organised a series of fund raising events to raise a set amount of money. I went onto to run a magazine for patients as I felt strongly that there was no publication where they could 'have their say'. I applied to the Prince's Trust and was awarded a grant to set it up . . . . the more I thought about it the more I realised that I had moved away from my inner strengths and desires and also my natural abilities.

I started to allow myself to dream and visualise what I really wanted.

This lead me on a whole new exciting journey. When I had sat in front of my Counselling tutor, thinking, 'I want to do what you are doing'. Somewhere that manifested in my body and I 'believed' I could. I used to find myself thinking these thoughts every time I attended any course or workshop. I wanted to BE the trainer or facilitator.

I began writing workshops on personal development and visualised myself in the position of running them.

I have realised that there have been many times in my life when I have manifested what I wanted just by putting out the thought and then visualising it happening.

Some months after I had left the agency as a training co-ordinator and set up independently I was going through a quiet period as my personal life had hit a crisis. My marriage was crumbling, I felt stuck and I desperately wanted to change my life.

I felt so 'bored' so to speed things up a bit I began asking the universe to 'Jerk my life'. I don't know where those thoughts came from, but I do know I was so ready for 'action' of any kind!

Then I received a phone call from an emergency services organization which I had joined some months back. I was asked if I would go and work for 3 months in a warehouse on personal effects following an air crash abroad. It was the best thing I could have done at that time in my life. It was unusual to be sent for that length of time and my contract was expanded to 6 months.

At this time in my life I so needed distraction from my home and the universe responded to my plea. I was beginning to understand the saying: 'Be careful what you ask for.'

Hence, I'm now in NZ, alone and ready for whatever the universe wants to send my way. How exhilarating and so different from the me I used to be. The 'me' who always wanted to plan and know what was coming next.

I related to Amara in a lot of ways and being at Mana felt so perfect for me. I felt yet again I was being guided on my journey and Mana had provided me with a space to rest, evaluate and gently plan the next step forward without being too regimented.

After another superb meal at lunchtime I drove to the Coromandel town, which was about the same size as Raglan. I visited the local craft shops and bought a pair of Indonesian shorts, which looked like a skirt when worn, though when I sat down it completely opened up at the sides, so I had to be careful not to reveal too much! They would be ideal back home as well, though maybe not for work! I treated myself to a coffee and sat outside feeling very empowered by all that I had accomplished so far. Although it may not sound much I reminded myself that it is still unusual for a lady of my 'delicate age' to venture alone across the other side of the world for five weeks without knowing a soul there. So many comfort zones had already been stretched and I was fully aware of the inner growth that was taking place as a result, which I knew would benefit me when I returned home.

Today I realised that I didn't feel comfortable taking part in the 'New Spirit' event on Sunday in Auckland, as Wendy had suggested I do, so I decided to go and experience it instead. I telephoned Wendy and explained my feelings to her which she understood. Immediately I felt relieved, so knew I had made the right decision.

Tonight I experienced a full body massage in a little wooden cabin under the stars. It felt wonderful and was so needed after my mountain climb, which my poor heels were still suffering from! Well oiled and relaxed I retired to bed and allowed the essence of NZ to flow over me along with the oils!

Thurs 10th Feb 05

I woke at 7am refreshed and eager to greet the day. Breakfast at 8.30am followed by some writing and washing before venturing out to visit the Sanctuary, which was part of The Mana Retreat. It was about a twenty minute walk through the bush which once again was incredibly quiet except for the chatter of the cicadas. There were signposts along the way to prevent me from getting lost with some spiritual statues delicately placed along the route to greet me along the way. When I arrived at the top of the mountain the whole world seemed to open up to the incredible views of the Coromandel which were spectacular. The Sanctuary was an angular building with large windows facing the views. I opened the large heavy wooden door and once inside was aware of two young people enjoying the sacred space. One lay on her stomach writing in the middle of the floor while the other sat in silence appearing to be meditating. The energy was so alive and yet respectful of peace and quiet. I stayed for a while and walked around the stone path outside, which directed you back to where you came in. It was suggested that you think of something you want an answer to and walk round and see what happens. I'm not sure I found the answer but the walk was very relaxing! Once again I captured the mountain scenery on camera and finally walked back down through the bush. I knew it wouldn't be wise to attempt the mountain climb as my heels were still convalescing from my mountain climb with Bill on Monday!

Later I drove to Thames, the nearest large shopping centre and enjoyed a lazy stroll looking in the shops and treated myself to a chi latte, my latest favourite drink. It was enormous so I could only manage half. Eventually I drove back after buying some more CD's to play in the car: Andrea Bocelli and Ray Charles—that's better! I do enjoy music when driving. I stopped to have a paddle in the sea and collected some fabulous shells, some of which were gold aluminous and so delicately marked.

I came back to change into swim wear but when I went out again I realised there wasn't time to go all the way to the coast before dinner so went for another paddle instead in a harbour nearby.

Once again dinner was delicious—a variety of home grown, organic produce made into an array of colourful, appetising dishes that teased every taste bud I had.

Another relaxing day! Tomorrow—it's time to move on—that feels a bit daunting having become very comfortable at Mana. I reminded myself that this trip is not about being comfortable but more to do with exploring the uncomfortable areas that I have spent a life time denying.

Fri 11th Feb 05

I woke early again, about 7am and found that I was feeling quite vulnerable. I hadn't heard from Linda after texting her last night and realised I was getting a bit anxious and needing to hear from her. I tried to telephone but no answer so left a message. After breakfast I tried again and she was there. It was so good to talk with her, I was missing real connection with home.

I joined the group meeting where we all did a meditation holding hands and then picked cards. Mine were 'dreams' and 'deceit'. Not quite sure what that meant but felt it might have to do with being true to myself. I'm still finding it difficult to just 'be'. After the meeting I went to settle the bill and once again connected very well with Amara. I do feel we may come together again through our work so we took each other's e-mails and I left her my details.

BE OPEN

As I was going to my car I met a man and woman and lots of synchronicities happened. In meditation I had asked for guidance and not to feel alone as I was feeling vulnerable as I was about to set off on the next part of my journey, then Michael and Romero came along. We stopped to chat so naturally and exchanged what we needed. They were off to Vida—exactly where I was heading! He also had a stand at the New Spirit Festival on Sun and I even found out later, when we bumped into each other again that he had met a lady from Norwich and taken her on a Sacred Journey (similar to Wendy's). So many connections and his business involved delivering trainings, same as mine.

*How can **Lesson 6** relate to us in our life . . . .*

On My travels when I felt alone I asked for company and it soon appeared. When we want something we need to open up to allow it in. If we ask but don't believe we can have it, the universe responds to our doubt as that is what we are feeling. For example if I had asked for company but followed that with 'but I don't suppose I'm going to have it', that's exactly what I would have attracted. It took me a long time to truly understand how this lesson works. 'You get what you *focus* on'. As I reflected I realised that so often I've said I've wanted something but followed it with a negative thought or doubt. When I have remained fully open and 'expected' it to appear, it has.

A perfect example of this is . . . . during a visit to a dear friend in Scotland, we visited an art and craft shop. I spotted a beautiful print of a couple dancing tango, something I had never experienced, but as a dancer I immediately appreciated the passion that exuded from the picture. I turned to my friend Dulce and said 'Now, that's dancing.' She smiled and said 'Buy it, and put it in your cottage so you will attract it in'. At the time I thought it was quite amusing to imagine myself dancing as this couple were. However I was very drawn to buying the picture and so I did. After returning home, a friend visited me, who happened to be a Feng Shui consultant. I showed her the picture and she immediately said 'put it in a red frame and somewhere you will see it all the time'. I followed her suggestion and hung it in my office above my computer and hence found myself imagining more and more 'being' the lady in the picture. It really should be no surprise, to all you believers out there that within 2 weeks I had an email about tango classes in Norwich. I had never heard of tango in my area before! I'm sure I don't need to tell you that I enrolled on the class and the rest is history. Tango became my passion and although I may not dance it in quite the poise of the lady in the picture I certainly have experienced the passion of the dance!!

So being open is simply allowing your dreams to become a reality. As the saying goes 'Be careful what you ask for' . . . . In other words are you ready to receive it?

*I invite you to explore **lesson 6** . . . .*

Being open is a truly wonderful way to live. It means you invite whatever is drawn into your life by listening to your body instead of your mind. If it *feels* right allow it, if it doesn't reject it. Quite a simple rule, so why not try it.

For a week record every time your body is attracted to something/ someone and even if you don't act on it just record it and do the same every time you feel negative about something/someone.

Your body never lies but your mind constantly plays tricks so when you learn to listen to your body signals and quieten your mind you will live a much easier and fulfilling life, You will start to experience what your heart desires, even though your mind may not have told you so.

After a week read back your findings and then explore when you did act and when you didn't. Soon you will learn the value of listening to your body, but this one needs practice if you want to have great results.

_____

_____

_____

_____

_____

_____

_____

_____

_____

ACCEPT

Today was very testing on the road. I intended to go and see Jamie and Michelle at Vida but lost my way and ended by going too far north. By the time I found out it was too late so I guess I was just not meant to go there today.

So instead I stopped at Coromandel town for a coffee and cake and bought another pair of shorts, the same as I bought the other day as they are so comfy. I then set out to find Trish at Cockle Bay near Auckland. Again I found myself lost but after a lot of stops and asking the way I eventually found her address, only to find she wasn't even there. Her son and friends greeted me and for one awful moment I thought I'd made a mistake. Luckily Trish soon returned and we then joined her sister and family at an Indian restaurant nearby.

I'm certainly learning to trust more and more and am panicking less when things don't turn out as I expected.

*How does **Lesson 7** relate to us in our life . . . .*

This lesson is also about letting go of 'control'. On my travels I had a plan and when it didn't appear to be going the way I'd expected I had two choices: To fight against what was naturally happening or to allow whatever was happening, to happen. It never ceases to amaze me that when I let go of trying to steer my life, it has a way of steering itself and always in a much calmer and better way. Being in a foreign country I obviously felt vulnerable at times and to allow my instinct and 'right' brain to lead me instead of my 'left' brain was sometimes a huge challenge. Self doubt and fear were always hovering near the surface. However the more I trusted my instinct the easier it became to let go the next time.

It's like trying anything new, we have to practise to get better and trusting your instinct is no different!

When life is suddenly looking unsure and we feel tested the natural response is to 'panic' and immediately try to gain 'control'. Usually by doing these two things we just feed our insecurity and end up feeling much worse. So how about changing the natural tendency to 'solve the problem' and instead do nothing. This may feel totally irresponsible and very uncomfortable at first, but hey, if the other way wasn't working, why not give it a try!! As a counsellor and trainer, I teach students the art of 'accepting' and 'not solving' and they often comment on how they 'gain' control by doing just that.

So how does this work . . . . By accepting, we relinquish our power. It's similar to when a relationship is experiencing difficulties. We so often become defensive and react to our partner's emotions. By accepting and even forgiving we actually regain our power in the relationship. It's when we struggle to hold on or try to change the situation that we feel 'powerless'. The same thing applies to other areas of our life. When we feel unhappy about something and don't see a solution then acknowledge it and take a step back and allow the universe to step in and assist you. I always ask for help. I'm sure you've heard of the saying 'Ask and it is given' or 'Be careful what you ask for' Well it's true . . . I once asked 'Jerk my life' I was bored with the lack of movement in my life at that time and yearned for some action. Boy did that work!! I no sooner asked and shortly after received a telephone call from an Organisation that I was a member of for emergency disasters. It was the first deployment I was sent on and I ended up away for 6 months!!

It's also important to remember not to control the outcome when we ask for anything. Just send up the request and then accept it will come when and how the universe decides to give it.

Margaret, a client of mine was tired of dating 'losers' and decided to write down all that she required in the man of her dreams. She had reached a stage in her life where she was no longer willing to compromise important values that she felt needed to be present in a relationship in order for it to succeed. However, once she had written her 'manifesting list' of what this man needed to have, she then accepted that it would happen when and how the universe decided. She had also worked on her own personal development sufficiently to have reached a stage where she was completely at peace with being on her own and was prepared to allow the space needed for the 'right' person to appear and appear he did with all the credentials she had asked for!

I invite you to explore **lesson 7** . . . .

Make a list of things you would like to change in your life and write them in a positive way e.g. *Have a job that fulfils me and pays me adequate money to live a life doing all the things I love.*

When you have written your list, ask the universe to take care of it for you.

Put the list somewhere safe and then ask for obvious signs, so you will know when to make the right moves toward your dream(s). Be patient, it may take a little longer than you want but it will work if you remain in a constant state of expectation and trust. However if you allow negative thoughts to dominate you will change the vibration and invite a different outcome.

I really do encourage you to try this one, as once you have experienced a positive result you will definitely be repeating the exercise many times in your life and as a result you will live your life in a truly intuitive way.

I know this may sound very strange to some of you but there are forces out there that we do not understand but the evidence is there to show us that this exercise does work and frequently has for me. Do make sure you write what you want in a positive way as if you already have it e.g. I have a wonderful new home . . . . *not ' I wish I had a wonderful new home', otherwise you will just remain wishing instead of getting.*

_____

_____

_____

_____

_____

_____

_____

_____

_____

Sat 12th Feb 05

Trish escorted me to the conference centre at Waipuna, near Auckland where I met up with Wendy, Kayla and others. It was a day called 'Vision Saturday' learning about 'Mannatech' which is a supplement from Texas. It seems to have given those who have taken it, a new lease of life. I could certainly see the benefits especially when I heard the testimonials. Wendy and Kayla had already signed up to sell it and as it was a networking business, they were looking to recruit as well. I also found the seminar useful for tips on improving your business.

After, Kayla and I made our way to a friend's house for the evening, where we met up with Wendy and co again. Conversation flowed whilst we indulged in tasty delicacies.

Once back at Trish's I was ready for my bed and as Trish hadn't come home I decided to retire. She finally arrived back at 12.00 so I decided to join her for a chat and a coffee where we started to share a part of our lives with each other. Her sister and Rob turned up, albeit at a late hour and fresh coffee was on offering— but I declined as I was really feeling the effects of the day by now and wanted to get an early start.

Sun 13th Feb 05

Once washed, dressed and basic needs attended to Trish offered to drive me to the 'New Spirit Festival' at Auckland. It was similar to the ones I had visited back home but on a much larger scale. They had 4 seminars every hour from 9am-7pm, which were attended by 50-100 people at a time. It was very interesting and I really enjoyed dipping into the different subjects and promoting my own work in England.

Wendy was helping an astrologer friend on her stand and as I was fascinated with the subject I decided to go to her talk. I was amazed at how accurate she seemed to be, listening to the feedback from people I knew there.

Trish came about 4pm to meet me so I could follow her home. 'I can't believe it', she said. 'I would never normally come to these events and the one I do come to I bump into an old friend who's just asked if I would film Brandon Bayes when she gives a talk in Auckland this week'. I was amazed and speechless. 'Why are you looking so surprised' she enquired. 'I composed myself as I told her 'Brandon

Bayes, was one of my mentors and had been a huge influence on me when I started my business five years ago. Reading Brandon's book 'The Journey' had been the starting point of me changing my whole life. I had decided to go on her intensive 2 day workshop in London. I couldn't believe she was out here the same time as I was. I had wanted so much to be involved in some of her work but until then wasn't sure how to go about it. I knew they took support workers who had already been on her 'Intensive' course' so this was a golden opportunity to follow through with another dream.

LESSON 8

EXPECT

Trish told me that she heard them saying that they wanted helpers who had completed that very course I had attended, for when Brandon moved onto Christchurch. Of course it was no coincidence that I was about to travel over to the South Island so would be making my way to Christchurch in time for when she arrived. Trish suggested I go to the stand that was advertising Brandon's work and ask for details. I didn't need to be told twice, but went straight off to find 'The Journey' stand. Once I found them I asked if they would like me to help when Brandon arrives in Christchurch, as I was intending to travel in that direction so could make sure I would be there when she arrived. They seemed keen and asked me to call the office on Monday, which of course I will. It does feel as if I'm meant to re-connect with Brandon Bayes!!! What timing, yet again the Universe shows how they will look after you if you just put out the intention and I was 'expecting' as it all seemed so 'meant to be'. I had been asking the universe to allow me to work with Brandon and often visualised what it would be like working with her, but I certainly had not tried to force it happening, just expected it!

Tonight was one of those nights that just unfolded. Trish and I talked and talked, consuming nearly two bottles of wine and chocolates!! Well it had to be soaked up with something and chocolate was a good option. It felt really good to share a part of our lives together and eventually we retired to our beds about 12.30am. I realised tonight how much I missed my dear friends back home and how little I had actually talked for quite a while, at least in any depth, as I do with my close friends. Tonight was like a release of feelings and maybe a little emotion as well and it felt safe to do that with Trish. I thanked her before collapsing into bed,

How can we relate **Lesson 8** *to our life* . . . .

When we 'expect' we send out wonderful vibes of energy that give the message 'I'm open to whatever' and the responses we get can be so exciting. If we doubt that we will have what we yearn for, then we probably won't. The doubts block us allowing it in.

In NZ I expected the unexpected all the time. I often started the day totally open to any new experience that presented itself to me and because I was open I was also more aware, which meant I didn't miss them when they appeared. So when Trish told me about Brandon Bayes I felt grateful to be able to experience something I certainly had dreamt of for a long time but not tried to *make* it happen.

I also never forget to thank the universe for sending these golden opportunities for more personal growth.

I invite you to explore **lesson 8** . . . .

Look at your list of what you want to bring into your life and then spend some time dreaming about them. Try just one at a time so you can really focus on it. Give the dream as much detail as you can and then add some energy to it. Imagine what it would be like *living* your dream. Before you go to sleep, invest some time in adding detail to your dream. Make it as colourful as you can and most importantly *expect* it to become your reality.

This is the next important step to bringing your dream into your conscious state. Allow the right brain to work and give the left brain some time off. Record your findings here:

Mon 14ᵗʰ Feb 05

Valentines Day and no one to send a card to!!!

I telephoned Dympna, a dear friend, knowing that Lynne and Ann, more dear friends were going round to celebrate her birthday with her which was on 13th Feb but with the time difference it meant I would catch her on the right day. I hoped she hadn't switched the answer phone on and I was lucky she hadn't. She was so surprised to hear my voice and we had a lovely chat before passing me on to talk to Lynne and Ann. When I connected with voices I recognised I realised how much I missed familiarity, but I also knew that I must make the most of this amazing opportunity that I had given myself.

Trish led me to the southern bypass and I headed off South for Taupo.

At 4pm I arrived, after a short stop for lunch, when I went to the Tourist Information and booked the ferry for Thurs to cross over to the South Island.

Tonight I was staying at a Retreat Centre called Tauhara and managed to get a self-contained unit. It was situated high up with a scenic view. The energy was so different to Mana and once again I felt very alone. There was no catering here which meant a trip back to town to buy some food, then after exploring the grounds and taking some photos, I retreated to my rooms and settled in for the night. It was good to re-engage with my own thoughts and energy after having spent some time with people who had welcomed me so warmly into not only into their homes but part of their lives as well.

Tuesday 15th Feb 05

Mums birthday.

I left Tauhara at 10.30am after a good night sleep. The centre had been very quiet as there were no courses running at present but I could imagine it would be quite 'buzzy' when filled with people.

While in Taupo I went to find Huka Falls, which had been recommended to me as a good sightseeing spot. The waterfalls mirrored down the rocks, falling at such speed and landing with a deafening splash. Water was spilling in all directions and I sensed it cleansing my aura. As I breathed in nature and the splendour of my surroundings I walked along the bush track. I passed a couple on the way and after walking for a while and venturing further into the bush I became aware of feeling slightly vulnerable in my own company. This surprised me as being in the bush in NZ rarely caused that feeling in me, or others by what I'd heard. However as I always respected my intuition, I decided to set back.

When I really trusted, things would work out ok, they did and I recognised that I was doing this more and more . . . .

TRUST—THINGS WILL TURN OUT THE WAY THEY ARE MEANT TO

While walking alone today I began to feel vulnerable, so decided to turn back. I met a couple walking the direction I had just turned back from. 'Did you reach the end' they enquired. 'No', I smiled. 'I began to feel a little vulnerable on my own so decided to turn back'. They smiled at me warmly, 'Why don't you join us then.' 'I'd love to' and so we completed the walk together.

Ian and Allison were from Perth, Australia. They were visiting their daughter while also doing 4 weeks exploring. They invited me to join them back at their caravan and have a dip in a hot spa, which was perfect after our long trek. We exchanged contact details and waved goodbye as I set off for Napier. I had not booked accommodation and realised I was leaving it a bit late in the day when I arrived at 5pm. However I knew it would be ok and felt very drawn to take the chance and found a lovely Motel, a new experience! I managed to buy some food nearby and did a load of washing and settled in for the evening and even watched TV for a change.

Great day—and so good to let it just happen! I think I may be doing a lot more of that on the South Island!

AND . . . another synchronicity . . . the present I sent for Mum's birthday actually arrived on that very day!! I certainly couldn't have done that all on my own. I thanked the universe for timing it so perfectly!

How can we relate **Lesson 9** *to our life . . . .*

A very significant lesson to me as it takes me back to my powerful dream which I had soon after starting my own business . . . .

I was standing in an aeroplane by an open door, looking out at the expanse of sky surrounded by clouds. Everything inside me wanted to jump, but fear held me back. As I was feeling the fear a voice spoke softly from behind me, 'Trust', it whispered. I immediately felt safe and jumped. Flying through the sky I felt liberated, but that feeling was soon replaced by fear again. All sorts of thoughts ambushed my mind 'How will I land', 'Will I get hurt' 'Where will I be' and more . . . No sooner was I aware of these thoughts, a voice from behind once again whispered 'Trust'. Again my fear was replaced by a 'knowing' that I was safe and I landed safely. I found myself in the middle of a large field and quickly fear jumped in with thoughts of 'Am I safe', 'What if there's a bull in here' and no sooner these thoughts invaded my brain the voice from behind once again repeated 'Trust'. I never questioned that voice, it simply took my fear away and once again I found myself walking safely out of the field. I was now on a woodland path and felt the fear creeping back as it was quite dark and felt a bit eerie. However I kept walking and noticed a little gipsy looking woman sitting back amongst the trees. I couldn't see her face but as I walked passed her the voice said 'Go back and see her'. I sensed that she had something to tell me. I didn't even hesitate and knew at this point in my dream that whatever she told me I would be ready to do. Trust had proved its worth and I didn't need to question it anymore!

We have to give our 'inner voice', 'higher self', 'instinct', 'intuition' or whatever you feel comfortable calling it, a chance to prove that it does work. We also need to be patient and practise using it, so we will recognise it more and more. I'm always stating 'It's like using a new muscle and without regularly using it you cannot expect it to keep working well. Practise makes perfect, don't they say!'

In NZ although I felt tested I did sense that I would be alright, having not booked a bed at a holiday park I ended up in a very comfortable B&B which actually made a pleasant change!

I invite you to explore **lesson 9** . . . .

Plan an event or outing and then let go of the outcome. Trust it will turn out the way it's meant to. In other words do not keep your finger on the control button. If and when things start to go in a direction that you didn't anticipate—do not immediately try to change it, just wait and give yourself a chance to feel if this is how it's *meant* to be. You will probably feel uncomfortable at first, but try to recognise the difference between 'what is meant' and 'what needs action'. We so often act on an uncomfortable feeling instead of allowing it to 'talk' to us. If we allow our mind chatter to quieten we will 'feel' the right way to move forward. Of course we are bound to make mistakes when we are learning this lesson, just as we do when we exercise our other muscles. Sometimes we overdue it and then suffer the consequences. When we become more aware of our bodies we respect them and the same applies with our intuition. As we get in touch with that part of us we learn to respect it and doubt it less and less. This is such an important lesson so practise it well and I promise you will be delighted with the results.

Record your planned event/outing and then after the event record the outcome both with the event and your approach to it.

_____

_____

_____

_____

_____

_____

_____

_____

_____

Weds 16th Feb 05

After my very civilised stay at the Motel it was time, once again
to move on. I had caught up with e-mails and even phoned Mum,
knowing it was the eve of her birthday and as hoped had timed it
when my brother Howard and his family were there so had a chat
with Mum and Howard which felt really good. I find it amazing
that I can hear those back home so clearly, when I am so many
miles away. Personally I don't believe it's all down to technology
as we accept so much without really questioning 'how or why'

I learned that the weather was grim back home, so I could feel the
envy oozing out of my brothers voice as I told him what glorious
weather I was enjoying!

I managed to find a beach before leaving Napier but it was shingle so I just had a walk and then set off for Wellington. After about 1hr on the road I saw what looked like a lovely eating place so pulled in but when I realised the car park was full I tried to back onto the road just outside, then felt the car descend into a dip and once again felt so alone in dealing with it. Then another angel came to my rescue (in the disguise of a man!) and very kindly guided me out. We are never truly alone—never!!

Abbotslee was set in lovely gardens and the perfect place to replenish myself. It was a self service bar and you could have as much as you wanted, so I filled a plate with a variety of salads and found a sunny spot in the garden to enjoy both the food and the surroundings.

There have been times on this journey that I would so dearly have loved to have company to share my experiences with and this is of one of them. Isn't it strange that when I'm alone I'm so aware of couples everywhere. I know I can cope with my own company and at times prefer it but nothing can be quite as good as the intimacy between two souls who really connect in a special way. This journey is helping me to understand what it is I am really wanting in my life. Space to be my own person but in a relationship that can allow two individuals to share enough time together to enjoy a special bonding.

There is something so welcoming about this country and this solitary journey feels completely right at this time in my life. It is also giving me lots of time to think with no interruptions or responsibilities pulling at me, a luxury I knew little about a few years ago.

LESSON 10

PACE IT

I drove into Wellington, which seemed to take forever and I began to feel vulnerable. The journey had taken from 11.00am to nearly 6pm with two stops, which I desperately needed as I was feeling so weary. The concentration needed on these roads takes more of my energy than I had anticipated. I hated approaching the traffic especially when it was 'rush hour'. I drove to where the ferry crossing was so I would have some idea of where to go tomorrow . . . then realised it was getting late to find somewhere to stay!

Motels were showing 'No Vacancy' so I drove to a Holiday Park and managed to get a basic kitchen cabin, which meant sharing toilets/showers.

I went for a drive to find the local supermarket and was once again tested on my lousy sense of direction. I stopped and had a walk along the beach and felt quite tearful from the strain of the day. After allowing my thoughts to get in touch with my emotions I accepted how I felt and went to the supermarket, bought some food, settled in for the rest of the evening and had an early night in preparation of the early start I had planned for tomorrow

*How did **Lesson 10** relate to our life . . . .*

There were occasions on my journey when I didn't feel I gave myself enough time resulting in me feeling really vulnerable. Not being able to find a place to stay that night certainly pushed a few buttons.

By giving ourselves time we can act more from 'knowing' than 'panic'. Simple planning, but allowing things to change if required, will help us to work with our intuition more comfortably. If we act in haste we may be listening to fear instead of our intuition.

*I invite you to explore **Lesson 10** in your life . . . .*

When we are young we are often impatient as we have not learnt the skill of waiting and allowing. However as we mature many of us appreciate the value of patience and as a result learn to live more at peace. 'What will be, will be' rings true for many of us just as 'time is the essence'.

This lesson was a huge one for me and I'm constantly reminded of it when I witness the anxiety of others who are still learning from it. If only I could prevent them from going through the feelings of despair that I have experienced, but I can't. The best lesson we can give others is to 'live by example' what we've learnt and not preach or try to control the outcome for those who are not yet ready to learn it. It will most likely push them further away from discovering the answers for themselves. When we walk our own talk we will attract others to follow, without force.

Record when you have felt impatient, acted too quickly, or tried to control another's actions. What was the result from your behaviour and how do you think you could have acted differently.

_____

_____

_____

_____

_____

_____

_____

_____

_____

_____

LESSON 11

STAY CALM

I realised I didn't have an alarm clock (at least not one I could work, as I had brought a new one and I couldn't work the technology!), so it meant I really had to TRUST that I would wake early enough to get going for the ferry crossing. I was so aware of this concern and didn't trust enough to stay calm so I woke every half hour from 3am until I finally needed to get up at 6am!

*How did **Lesson 11** relate to our life . . . .*

Staying calm is the only way to be able to hear your 'inner voice'. I began to panic about waking up in time and as a result woke every 1/2hour from 3am onwards. This actually did prove I didn't need to worry at all as my body had programmed what I was telling it. Unfortunately due to my panic it over responded!

Do remember to practise ways of calming your mind as well as your body.

*I invite you to explore **Lesson 11** in your life . . . .*

_____

_____

_____

_____

_____

_____

_____

_____

_____

_____

Thurs 17th Feb 05

Once on the road I thought I was more comfortable with the route to the ferry until I took a wrong turning and then had to stop and ask. Fear started to raise its ugly head once again but I was soon back on track and felt so relieved when I was finally in the queue. Then to my surprise Allison and Ian appeared in the same queue. How lovely it was to see them again and how amazing was our timing! We shared some of the 3hr trip together.

Once we arrived at Picton it was a lot easier getting off the ferry than getting on. I headed for Nelson, my first port of call and decided that I should look for accommodation first. It was very booked up everywhere but luckily (or was it?!!) I timed it right to get the last single cabin, with sharing toilets and showers in another holiday camp. Once booked in I set off to explore the area before returning to catch up with some e-mails and settling in for an early night.

Fri 18th Feb 05

REMEMBER THE HARE AND THE TORTOISE

I'm learning to live in my own space so much better, which I feel is a result of all this time alone.

Where is the time going? I thought being on my own it would drag, but not a bit of it, it's flying by. It's probably because I have to keep sorting out where I'm going, what I'm going to eat and accommodation and it seems to take all day to do just that. I need to find an easier way or do I?

I'm writing this after a glass of wine and feeling a bit tipsy, as I've only had some crisps—so I'm not sure if details are going to be correct! Hiccup!!

Well I left Nelson after exploring the shops and getting a bit lost while looking for my car, but what the hell, I found it eventually. I'm so impressed with myself as my bearings are not good, but I'm actually getting to places all be it a little longer than if I was with a man, who always seem so 'bloody' perfect at knowing where to go!!!

*How does **Lesson 12** relate to our life . . . .*

In my case not so much a hare and tortoise but a man and a woman! I may not have had a good sense of direction and may have travelled many more miles than I needed to, but I always arrived at my destination in the end!

Does it matter how or when you travel on your personal development journey? No, what does matter though is that you do it in your own way and in your own time. We so often strive to be like others or please others and even try to keep up with others, when all that is important is that we find our own unique way which will be valuable to us.

*I invite you to explore **Lesson 12** in your life . . . .*

When have you tried to race against time to get something done only to make mistakes or miss the whole essence of what you were doing?

Next time you rush to achieve something stop for a moment and question why you have put yourself under time pressure. Is it to please someone, prove to yourself you can do it or maybe you have just developed the habit of rushing through life at top speed?!!

I challenge you to 'slow down' and make note of what you notice as a result. Did it actually make a big difference in the end and how did you feel within yourself by allowing yourself time.

LESSON 13

PLAN AHEAD WITHOUT ATTACHMENT

Having arrived at Motueka, south of Nelson I think I've cracked it, yes really I have!!

These holiday parks are ideal but you do need to book ahead if you want decent 'facilities'. At my delicate age I do appreciate having them, so when I arrived here I actually planned ahead and joined the club in order to get discount. Having said that I am treating myself to a B&B tomorrow night—a girl should have a treat once in a while!

Now I feel so much better having booked 4 nights ahead, knowing that I can change any of them if I choose. It's given me peace of mind and as I've been going by my intuition all the time this felt absolutely right as I do need reassurance that I'm safe as well.

*How does **Lesson 13** relate to our life . . . .*

Yes folks, I finally cracked it . . . to plan ahead without attachment, which immediately brought peace of mind. If we have a fluid plan, allowing the universe to throw in any changes if it chooses, we will then remain calmer and are far more likely to allow ourselves to take risks. It may sound strange but it's true, at least for me it is! As we relax into allowing our lives to flow naturally we invite change to visit us.

I ventured into Motueka, which was only a 5min walk and bought some supper with a top up on the wine of course! When I returned I treated myself to a 1/2hr in the hot spa—beautiful, and so unwinding. Back to my cabin and a glass of wine was next on the agenda. *I'm actually looking after myself and nothing wrong with that!!*

I invite you to explore **Lesson 13** . . . .

Look at your life plan, if you have one and decide what you want to bring into your life and then imagine throwing it high up into the universe offering it up to be sorted. It is no good attaching your dreams to specific people or even places as that is almost certainly going to invite disappointment in. Be very specific about what you do want and allow the universe to find it for you—much more fun!!

You may know someone who has all the qualities that you would like in a person. Write them down and imagine someone coming into your life with those qualities. It may well be the same person, but the chances are it will be someone you have never met who matches equally as well.

This also encourages us to dream positively and our thoughts are very powerful. There is so much evidence to show that we can bring into our live what we think about. Therefore we must be careful not to latch negative thoughts onto the end of our dreams . . . . if we dream 'I'm going to find a partner who has the same interests as me and who is fun to be with' and then add on the end 'but I don't suppose I will' then that is the part that will probably come true, because that is what you truly believe and are focusing on.

I once said to my daughter, when she was young, 'You can have anything you want, all you have to do is want it enough' and she now reaches for things many wouldn't, because she believes in herself and the power of thought. The key to achieving is believing!

_____

_____

_____

_____

_____

_____

_____

_____

_____

_____

Sat 19ᵗʰ Feb 05

LESSON 14

BECOME YOUR BIGGEST FAN!

I seem to be having vivid dreams during my travels and some they are quite easy to analyse or even significant to what's going on for me at the time. It seems that I have travelled to the other side of the world to discover what is deep inside me. The longer I'm away the more comfortable I am getting with my own company, sometimes to the point of not wanting anyone in my space at all. As I value myself more and more I become far more *reluctant to just fill time with anyone that happens to come along. Dare I say after 50 years I'm actually allowing myself to get to know **me** and am enjoying what I am discovering? I've found I talk to myself more and give myself a pat on the shoulder when I overcome obstacles like finding the car after losing my way in town only to discover that I was in the wrong car park! It's so good not to have to worry about what a fool I am, because it's only me and I allow myself to make mistakes and get over them. I'm even aware of laughing with myself and have realised that my higher self has really connected with me.*

What a day this turned out to be!!

As I sit on a beautiful deserted beach on Golden Bay I can count on one hand how many people there are. I think I must have died and gone to heaven . . . I'm surrounded by glorious white sands and the water, though chilly initially, was well worth the dip, it is so beautifully calm and so clear!

*How does **Lesson 14** relate to our life . . . .*

Who better to have as your biggest fan than yourself! Like the saying goes 'How can you expect someone to love you if you don't love yourself?' This is so true and makes such a difference to how others feel about you. If you go out happy with yourself, you radiate an energy that says 'I'm ok' and others will naturally be drawn to you. We all want to spend time with people who are positive and like attracts like, so if you are in a positive space, chances are you will attract the same your way!

*I invite you to explore **Lesson 14** . . . .*

Give yourself a day or at least part of a day, when you are going to treat yourself as a really 'special person'. Lighten up and see the funny side of what you do and give yourself a break. Look at yourself in the mirror at the beginning of the day and talk kindly. Ask yourself what you would like to do and listen back when you answer.

Try to spend as much of this day on your own, maybe treating yourself to going somewhere you really like. Enjoy a lunch at a favourite café. Perhaps take yourself off to the cinema or rent a DVD and treat yourself to a favourite meal. Whatever you do make sure it's just for you. At the end of the day, spend some time reflecting on how it felt to pamper yourself and write it down. The more you allow yourself to indulge in this exercise the higher your self esteem will be. If you find it difficult or have loads of excuses why you can't do it then I would question where is your self value and be aware that we all need 'time out' if we are not to experience 'burn out', which can come from physical, mental and emotional overload. It can creep on us when we least expect as we can be so absorbed in getting it right for everyone else that we fail to recognise the signs.

_____

_____

_____

_____

_____

_____

_____

_____

_____

_____

VALUE EVERY CONNECTION

Today I started by going to an open day at a Health & Well-being clinic in Motueka. There I met a variety of therapists and one I really connected with was Ijhan (that's a man!) We talked for what seemed like hours and shared our travelling stories. He originated from Holland and kindly gave me more contacts that I may, or may not want to follow through. It's wonderful when two strangers connect in a way that makes them feel that they already know each other. Maybe we did, in another life.

I sampled a Reflexology treatment from Ijhan and a Reiki Healing from another therapist. It was just what I felt I needed and boosted me so I felt ready to continue my travels.

After this invigorating dose of natural remedies I took to the road and headed toward Takaka where I had booked a B&B. I stopped on the way at a viewpoint and ended up having another hike through the bush to find it—it was worth it—if only for more photos!!

Next stop was at the 'Ngarua Caves' which were situated 2000feet above sea level and on the Takaka hill, where I had a chance to go on a tour down one of the caves. I had timed it perfectly. The marble found on Takaka hill is one of the oldest calcium carbonated rocks in NZ at an age of 450,000,000 years old.

As our tour guide carefully lead us down to what felt like walking into a science fiction film, we were enveloped in a cool damp atmosphere. I was in awe of the formation of stalagmites and stalactites all around us. Our imaginations ran wild as our Guides' humour encouraged us to see beyond. He informed us that weddings had even taken place down there. When he turned the lamps off an eerie dark stillness engulfed us and I imagined for a moment how scary it would feel to be alone down there.

Back on the road after an interesting tour with a very interesting Guide . . . next distraction was Pupu Springs, which I was recommended to see by one of the locals who said it was 'one of the jewels of Golden Bay'. It was very picturesque and once again quite a walk through the bush. The springs were so clear; I have never seen water like it.

It always feels so strange walking through the bush in this country and not feeling vulnerable, as everywhere is so deserted and even sitting on a desolate beach felt safe on this land. Everywhere felt so friendly and inviting.

I finally arrived at my destination 'The Garden Retreat' B&B, owned by a very friendly couple called Diane & Alan. It was definitely the best accommodation that I had stayed in so far or probably ever will on this trip, as it was quite a bit more expensive. I felt like a treat tonight and was so glad it was here. I had my own bathroom, balcony and even dressing room. It was surrounded by a lovely garden and only 7mins from the beach which was my first calling and where I began to write this entry!!

*How does **Lesson 15** relate to our life . . . .*

In NZ I learned to value every connection as I may not see these people ever again and as I believe in synchronicities I always value each person that I was lucky enough to encounter, knowing there must be a reason we met, even if it was simply to assist me on my journey.

Each person we meet, however brief, comes into our lives for a reason, season or life time and when you know which it is you know what to do with it. I had some words given to me which started by saying just that and I soon learnt the significance of them. So value every connection you make as you never know what lessons they bring you, never mind where the connection may lead you to.

*I invite you to explore **Lesson 15** . . . .*

Think about the people you have met in the last few months or longer and decide if there was a reason they came into your life. It may have been to give you information you needed, or to tell you something you needed to hear, or even teach you a lesson you needed to learn. Make note of any of your findings and keep a record of every new person you encounter that has had an effect on your life. You may be surprised to discover that you are meeting people for reasons you were not previously aware of and suddenly your encounters with new people become more meaningful, even the negative ones. It is usually when we are feeling uncomfortable that we are leaning our biggest lessons, so rather than be quick to complain about someone, perhaps it might be worth exploring why they may have come into your life. The quicker we learn the lesson, the less likely we are to repeat it with another.

_____

_____

_____

_____

_____

_____

_____

_____

_____

_____

_____

BE EMPOWERED

I decided it was time to go out on the town on my own and it was a Saturday night!

After I had freshened up, I put my glad rags on (first time this holiday) and ventured to the local hot spot, a restaurant I had been recommended called 'Muscles'. It was typically rustic and attracted the locals, which is exactly why I wanted to sample it. The food was delicious, I had a vegetarian lasagne with salad and a baked potato, which was mashed and served with soured cream. I was ready for this and realised I hadn't really eaten very well lately, healthy but nothing special, so this was really appreciated.

I felt so empowered to be dining out alone on a Saturday night and once again feeling ok about doing it! After I had eaten and enjoyed the ambience I went back to town to a bar where they served food and coffee as I knew a pianist would be playing there. It was practically empty and I enjoyed listening to the music as I sipped my cappuccino before returning to my 'posh' B&B where I retired to my 'lush' bedroom. It was a good Saturday evening out on the town alone!

How did Lesson 16 relate to our life . . . .

When I decided to go out alone on a Saturday evening, it felt quite challenging. At home I would never have done that. Why? Perhaps in case I saw someone I knew and then would feel self conscious at being alone. Also, at home I would have felt nervous about being out on the busiest night alone. However in NZ I did not experience any of these feelings and by venturing out alone I discovered just how empowering it was. To sit in a busy pub and eat alone and feel truly comfortable in my own skin, was definitely a new experience that I was ready to embrace.

In order to gain this feeling of empowerment it is essential that we stretch our comfort zones, albeit a little at a time . . . A friend of mine would take a book or newspaper with her when she wanted to dine alone, so she wouldn't feel so conspicuous sitting alone. For her it took away any embarrassment and meant she didn't miss out on going to the places she used to go to when she had a partner. I tried this and agreed totally with her. It suddenly opened up the possibility of visiting venues I had denied myself since being alone.

In NZ I felt freer to explore this and soon realised that other people are far too pre occupied with their own lives to give much attention to me.

*I invite you to explore **Lesson 16** . . . .*

Dare to stretch your comfort zones by planning an outing all by yourself. Make sure it's somewhere you really want to go and then go. Don't forget to take something with you like a book or magazine, if it's somewhere you may feel conspicuous.

Record how you feel before you go and then after and remember after you've dared to do it once it will get easier. Remember to smile at strangers so they will feel you are approachable and then they will be far more likely to greet you warmly in return.

_____

_____

_____

_____

_____

_____

_____

_____

_____

_____

Sun 20th Feb 05

I woke surprisingly early (as I didn't retire until gone midnight) to a beautiful sunrise at 6.30am and managed to capture it on camera. I'm so glad I invested in a good camera, that's easy to use and light to carry around. I've been able to download regularly onto my laptop, thanks to my dear brother! Linda and I were definitely right in thinking I should bring my laptop, it has been wonderful and I've been writing every day, which has felt so good. Reconnecting with my writing, something I always loved doing but have neglected for far too long. Ellie, you were also right when you told me to write more!! I am truly blessed with some very intuitive friends!

I found it difficult to return to 'slumber' so enjoyed absorbing the peace and tranquillity of this gorgeous room with cream and lemon decor. It reminded me of my own cherished bedroom back home. For a moment I felt homesick, but reminded myself that I would be back there before I knew it and would probably be yearning for where I am now, so I really must enjoy every minute of every day. I would not allow myself to negotiate on this and most of the time it has not been difficult to do!

I finally got my act together and enjoyed breakfast on the veranda. The German men who had also been staying had already moved on so I was not to enjoy the pleasure of their company. I doubt whether I missed much, as when I returned last night and went into the dining room, which was pitch black I was greeted by a deep voice and then spotted a man sitting drinking wine in the dark! I asked if it was ok to put the light on and he said 'yes' but offered no further conversation. I made a cup of tea and tried to initiate an exchange of words but he was not very forthcoming so I made a quick exit. Another beauty of being on my own, I don't have to put up with bad company.

Sunday breakfast, alone on the veranda felt just fine!

When I went downstairs Alan and Diane, the owners, asked if I would like to have a coffee with them before I departed. I did enjoy their company and realised that what I sometimes missed from being on my own was good conversation. They pointed me in the right direction for the 'hot spots' of Golden Bay and I set off to find them.

First I ventured further north to Collingwood and onto the beach of Wharariki, which they recommended. When I parked the car I could see I would have to walk a distance and noticed that others were putting jackets on—why?!! It was a lovely hot day!! I thought they must know something I don't so decided to follow my instincts and do the same. On went my hat, as it seemed extra windy and as I walked and walked for what seemed for ever I realised 'Windy Wellington' had nothing on this place. I doubt whether I would have had any hair left if it wasn't for the hat! At times I thought I was going to take off!

Once the beach was in view it was breathtaking (have I used that analogy before—I think so and will again and again in this country I'm sure!) It looked like a desert, with the sand blowing at such a force that I had to turn my head. It felt like sandpaper hitting my legs! I managed with great difficulty to walk to the sea and paddle but the force of the wind was very challenging. Once gain another deserted beach, except for one or two brave walkers who I gradually lost sight of.

It was quite an extraordinary view, but not somewhere to sit and chill. Unfortunately due to the extra strong winds this favourite haunt of seals meant none were to be seen.

I drove back to Collingwood and visited another couple of beaches, Puponga and Pakawau but they were also isolated and it meant walking a long way to the sea so on this occasion I decided to keep moving. I called in at a local artist's exhibition; it's always good to see local talent—if only!!

I made my way back to Motueka as I needed to get back there tonight to head west tomorrow. I stopped at Bencarri to visit a nature park where they had tame eels! I fed all the animals and then walked down to the Anatoki River with sticks and food (blancmange & mince) just as I learned Maggi McCallum did 90 years ago with her sister, Edna. Little did they realise when they started doing it that one day it would be a tourist attraction! The eels were fascinating and came out of the water to take the food from the sticks as you offered it to them.

Unfortunately the battery in my camera had died which meant no photos this time! However I had already captured most of the animals!

Another great day—I drove on to Motueka and this time had a motel cabin with kitchen and en-suite. That's better! I'm really getting this sorted now, especially if I can think ahead and book what I want.

I was shattered and just lay on the bed and watched 'Spiderman' on TV. I'd never seen it before and actually surprised myself by enjoying it.

Mon 21st Feb 05

I woke quite a lot last night and didn't feel great but recovered quickly as I prepared to travel on. Once on the road I headed for Westport, but kept going wrong and ended up on one of those treacherous, gravel mountain roads—scary!

LESSON 17

RECOGNISE YOUR ANGELS (IN DISGUISE)

As I drove on the treacherous road I began to feel vulnerable and asked for guidance . . . I soon spotted a man sitting in his van in a lay by and he pointed me in the right direction. He even seemed to follow me down in his truck, which made me feel looked after until I finally hit a metal road again and at the junction he wound down his window and asked me if I had enough fuel. It was very thoughtful of him and I thanked him and we departed in opposite directions. The universe is certainly looking after me!

On route I bought some strawberries and plums from a man who originated from Essex but had been in New Zealand since 1959.

Further on route I spotted the 'Adventure & Heritage Park' at the Buller Gorge. Sheepishly I entered and saw the chance to 'fly' across the swing bridge. I wavered for about 30mins on whether I would be brave enough to have a go. Everything inside me wanted to and I finally felt ready after two comments were said to me. One young lad said 'Live a little' and another said 'If you don't do it now, when you leave you will not have another chance as this is the only place you can.' That was enough and I kept thinking how I'm always telling others to take the risk so 'I should walk my talk' otherwise how can I expect others to. So I did the most daring pursuit of all 'Superman'—which meant being harnessed and running along a platform and allowing myself to fall into the air just as if I was flying. I've always wanted to experience the feeling of flying through the air and have always said if I had a chose to come back as anything I wanted I would be an eagle. To be powerful and free must be incredible.

How did **Lesson 17** *relate to us in our life* . . . .

In our life we meet many people, but sometimes when we least expect someone comes along and changes our life. They may say something, do something or even show you something which makes a difference for ever. Often it is not until much later that we recognise the impact that person made on our life. Some of these people have been described as 'Earth Angels in disguise'.

I invite you to explore **Lesson 17** . . . .

Reflect on people who have changed your life and write down how they did. Also think about how you may have changed another's life by any actions you have done and record your memories. What lessons have you learned from these experiences . . . .

_____

_____

_____

_____

_____

_____

_____

_____

_____

LESSON 18

WALK YOUR TALK

As I was harnessed I felt the adrenalin welling up inside and then I had to allow myself to fall off the bridge. That was difficult and TRUST really had to kick in . . . but when it finally did, it was phenomenal (or awesome as they say here!) Wow, wow, wow and photos and disc for evidence! EVERYTHING INSIDE ME SAID 'WALK YOUR TALK' AND IT WAS WORTH IT! Just like my dream had said 'TRUST' and when I did I allowed myself to fall from the aeroplane. I recognised the similarities between my 'real life' and my 'dream'.

Back on the road and making further headway to Westport. I finally arrived about 6pm and it was 5mins from the beach. I had a short walk to the sea before retiring after another full fun packed active day. Driving is tiring at times—but I so want to see as much as possible.

I've now heard back from 'The Journey' with Brandon Bayes and they do want me to work as a trainer this week-end so I've booked Fri, Sat, Sun and Mon at Christchurch. How exciting and we finish with a dinner with Brandon on Sun eve. To think 5 years ago I started my business after being influenced from reading her book! A lot has happened since then to both of us, I'm sure!

*How did **Lesson 18** relate to us in our life . . . .*

THE POWER OF INTUITION

So many people are good at telling others what to do, even though they often would never follow through with the same advice if it was thrown in their direction. I feel very strongly about 'don't dish out what you can't take' so this experience was truly a time when I felt tested on 'walking my talk'.

However when we do, we shift our focus and are then able to talk from experience, which is similar to talking about something we have a passion for. Talking from our heart as opposed to talking from our head is always received more positively. So the lesson here is to experience as much as you can if you want to assist others in their personal journeys.

I invite you to explore **Lesson 18** . . . .

Write an account of when have you learnt a valuable lesson from something you experienced? How did you use this lesson and whom did you help as a result?

_____

_____

_____

_____

_____

_____

_____

_____

Tues 22ⁿᵈ Feb 05

I left at 9am, which was good for me! I knew it would be a long drive to Haast and not much time to stop off though I did take a break at Pancake Rocks, which was really worth seeing. The incredible formation of rocks and no one can understand why it only happened there.

LESSON 19

SLOW DOWN

I also stopped at a small town to have a late lunch on the way to Franz Josef . . . I do wish I hadn't! It was at this point that I was glad I was a woman because a policeman stopped me for 'speeding'!! Oh no! Not with 9 points already on my licence!! My heart was in my mouth but he seemed quite compassionate and asked me loads of questions including what did I do for a living?!! I really played on the fact that I was a trainer and for the police! Please, please be kind to me, I prayed. He even asked if I was travelling alone to get over a marriage break up!!! I wanted to ask what that had to do with anything, but instead smiled sweetly and simply told him the truth 'No, not at all.'

Finally he let me off with a fine, half of what it should have been. So another $120 to pay out! That's the second fine I've had since entering this country—please don't let there be a third· SLOW DOWN!!

I drove on to Franz Josef, the home of all the glaciers. I would have loved to have seen them but they are a day's visit and it just wasn't a priority so onwards and upwards (literally at times!)

I finally drove into the Holiday Park I'd booked at Haast at 7.30pm—these journeys are always much longer than I expect. I've been on the road since 9am and apart from a few stops have been driving all the time. Once unloaded in a very comfortable self-contained unit, this time lounge/kitchen separate from bedroom, I then went to find the beach, which I wrongly assumed, was near. When I realised it was going to be another long drive I decided against and retired to my unit, did a wash load, which urgently needed doing, had supper and caught up with my journal and photos.

Another day came and went—where are they going and I'm becoming weary and a bit lonely from all the travelling. Never mind, come Friday I will meet up with other people involved in Brandon's week-end, which will be a pleasant change from spending so much time alone.

All this time in my own company allows me to think and evaluate my life and those in it! I've realised how much I value my dear friends and if I were to live in the best place in the world it still would not be enough if I didn't have those who are special to me nearby. As for that 'soul mate' stuff, I'm not sure, as I have no claims on a partner in my life at present. At times I ponder over a relationship that comes and goes. We seem to respond so well to each other and he understands me and seems to accept me for who I am but there always seems to be such limitations on our relationship that I try not to let myself get in as deep as I know I could and maybe would like. What a waste, my dear friend, because I so understand your need for freedom and not wanting commitment because it's within me too. To deny us what is so evidently there does not make sense sometimes especially as you are always there and never seem to really want to isolate yourself from what we have either. A puzzle I have not solved as yet!!

How did **Lesson 19** *relate to us in our life . . . .*

Boy did I need this lesson! I was always racing against time or filling every space I had. Why? I didn't know then, but looking back I recognise how space meant time to think and I wasn't ready to allow myself to do that, not to the depth I felt I might if time was the essence. As a result I have often nearly burnt out and having experienced that once I have no intention of repeating that lesson! As I always quote 'If you don't stop it, it stops you'. How true these words are.

I invite you to explore **Lesson 19** . . . .

Look at your life and identify if you give yourself time, just for you. If you don't then perhaps you could just allow enough time to write down the reasons you don't. Identify how important you are in your life and what different roles you play for those in your life.

It is usually when our 'self value' is low that we don't give ourselves this precious thing called time. So I do challenge you to perhaps find a way to introduce it if you feel it's lacking in your life. Also try slowing down in your daily routine and savouring the moment instead of rushing through the day as if it were a race.

Wed 23rd Feb 05

After a disturbed night due to constant itching on my left foot where I had been eaten alive by mosquitoes, I felt somewhat vulnerable and lonely this morning. Ok I just felt sorry for myself and no one was there to reassure me. THE SIGNIFICANCE OF ITCHING—RECOGNISE WHATS IRRITATING ME?!!

Last night I had a comfortable unit but felt very exposed as I was situated on a corner and was aware of everyone walking past. I didn't like the fact my lounge/kitchen were separate to my bedroom. Not to worry it was 7pm when I arrived so I wasn't going to be spending a long time here.

On the road 10am and in theory it should be a three and a half hour drive to Queenstown, but that's without a stop—and that just isn't going to happen is it?!!

The glaciers were beautiful and a good reason to pause and take photos.

LESSON 20

ALLOW THE FEELING

This morning I felt another shift had taken place in me. I no longer felt quite so exhilarated and energised. I was feeling quite lonely and in need of company, but not just any company, real soul connecting company. All those who I felt I had that connection with were the other side of the world, so I would have to pursue my journey of 'aloneness'. I telephoned Wendy and wasn't even meant to talk to her as her answer phone was on! WAS THIS A SHIFT OF ENERGY IN MY MOOD? Well it's ok to allow it.

I drove on, stopped for coffee and photo shots at Lake Hawea.

Another interesting stop was at Lake Wanaka where they had a Centre called 'Puzzling World'. I needed a bit of amusement so thought I'd stop and see what it was all about. There was a great maze—which they reckoned should take 1-2hrs to achieve. As my bearing is pretty bad normally why ever did I think I would be able to find myself out of a maze—correct, I couldn't and unless I wanted to still be trying tomorrow I had to finally admit defeat and sneak out of one of the emergency exits. It was no good following others as they were no better (men included!) which now makes me question my theory that men are better at sensing direction than women—apparently not in New Zealand!

I drove on once again witnessing spectacular scenery going through Lake Wanaka, finally arriving at Queenstown. Yes it was worth seeing, but not to stay more than one night as the shops consisted of sport, sport and more sport, either wear it or do it and if you're not doing it then there were plenty of restaurants full of others talking about it. I'd like to know what typical New Zealand food is—so far I haven't a clue!! It was good to ramble round the shops and not be driving for a change. I did some retail therapy, which perked me up a bit and then back to my room, to have supper. It was a good thing I bought forks and spoons as no facilities here!! The room is OK though and I don't feel exposed tonight so consequently feel more secure.

*How did **lesson 20** relate to us in our life?*

If you learn to 'listen' to your body you will recognise when there is a shift of energy which can be helpful in everyday life. You will begin to understand when it is necessary to allow yourself to experience the emotion you are feeling or when it is time to change it. You will also become more accepting of your feelings and emotions rather than deny them which can often result in burn out.

Listening to your body will make you more aware of others peoples energy and then you will know if their energy is what you want to be near or if it would be best to distance from them.

I invite you to explore **Lesson 20** . . . .

Record any times when you have been aware of a change in mood or energy which you can relate to another person or situation. How did your body tell you? What action did you take (if any)?

_____

_____

_____

_____

_____

_____

_____

_____

_____

_____

_____

_____

Thurs 24th Feb 05

The days are certainly flying by; I can't believe it's nearly the end of February already—though it does seem ages since I left the UK.

Up and on the road at 9.00am, heading towards Christchurch, but stopping tonight at Timaru. On the way to Cromwell I stopped to watch some bungee jumping and now I appreciate how brave my daughter Katrina and her friends were when they went on their travels and reported home with their latest dare devil adventures. It definitely was not for me.

I stopped for some wine tasting which was much more up my street! But it turned out to be wine 'smelling'—how disappointing was that, but probably just as well as I'm driving and I don't need to be stopped again!

Next stop for lunch at Omarama then back on the road . . . I met a Kiwi who was giving a Dutch girl and her bike a ride on his truck. We had stopped to admire the same view and shared a lovely conversation. I learnt another local word 'Choice' meaning the same as 'Sweetas' or 'that's great' in our language. After I left them I was reminded just how much I was missing conversation with people I felt I could connect with.

Next stop—Lake Tekapo, what a picture!

I arrived at Timaru about 4.00pm. I had been upgraded at the same price as someone had wanted to stay another night and they needed my original room. Not a problem, it must be the best deal yet!

A trip to the 'Quicksave' supermarket, and walk along the beach which was near, but nothing special, then back to base for an evening of journal writing, wine and supper.

Fri 25th Feb 05

IT'S OK TO FEEL VULNERABLE.

I heard there is snow at home; well I hope it's gone by my return!

I woke to a dull, cloudy start and found my mood was quite low too. I still feel quite weary so perhaps it would be best not to take the scenic route today as driving takes a lot of concentration. I still have a way to go and tonight I'll need to be fully alert when I join Brandon Bayes evening for trainers who are participating in her Intensive week-end of 'The Journey' at the Holiday Inn at Christchurch.

5.45pm and I'm sitting outside the Holiday Inn where in 45 minutes I will meet the other trainers on Brandon's weekend. I do feel vulnerable, though not sure why. Just lately I've felt these negative feelings more and more and think it may be to do with the 'aloneness' of my journey. BEING AWARE OF MY VULNERABILITIES WILL HELP ME TO EMPATHISE WITH OTHERS.

This weekend feels perfectly timed, as after feeling isolated I'm now going to be surrounded with people.

The evening was intensive as Brandon welcomed us and then shared with us the programme that we would be taking part in. It was quite surreal meeting Brandon. In her book 'The Journey' she shares how she discovered a tumour in her stomach, the size of a basket ball and how 6 weeks later after rejecting orthodox medicine and following a strict regime of natural, holistic medicine and treatment it totally vanished and she was cured. She created two programmes, an Emotional journey where you work through emotional layers and a physical journey where you are working more within your body where ever you are drawn to work. After reading her book I went to Brandon's Intensive 2 day training in London and was moved by the experiences I witnessed and also felt for myself. Having trained as a nurse and a counsellor I developed a hunger to know more about the body/mind connection and so my personal journey began. I invited therapists and teachers of many different subjects to talk and share their experiences with myself and others which naturally enhanced my own learning. So it felt quite amazing to now be meeting and working with Brandon on the other side of the world!

How did **Lesson 21** *relate to us in our life?*

Feeling vulnerable is part of living. It is quite normal to feel it from time to time, especially when we find ourselves in a new situation. A new relationship, new job, living in a new area, making new friends . . . . so many new experiences if we allow life to give them to us.

Why are they good for us? Because without them we would never grow and would instead resist change, giving out an energy of being completely in control, only most of us see right through it.

We've all met people like this. They are the ones who stay in the same job for years, making any newcomers feel very uncomfortable in their presence. Anyone who is confident in their own skin will soon recognise when someone is behaving in this way toward them and will be aware that it is only that persons own insecurity that is creating the problem. If we feel secure and confident with ourselves we have no need to patronise and bully others.

However, when we do find ourselves on the receiving end of this behaviour, it can be an opportunity to explore what has caused it and hopefully decide to change our response in some way or walk away from it.

Feeling vulnerable presents an opportunity to be kind to ourselves. Accept the feelings and then explore them. To be kind to yourself is a lesson in itself and is so empowering.

When I feel vulnerable in mind or body I immediately make a priority to look after myself. I will pamper myself and include some quiet time to allow whatever needs to be released, be released.

I invite you to explore **Lesson 21** . . . .

Spend some time reflecting on when you have felt vulnerable. Write about why you did and then what you did about it.

If you were to repeat that experience what do you think you would do about it now?

_____

_____

_____

_____

_____

_____

_____

_____

_____

TAKE THE RISK

My comfort zones were once again well and truly tested as I tried to absorb all that Brandon said, wondering if I was really up to being a support trainer as it's five years since I did the 'Intensive Programme' myself and I haven't really been practising 'The Journey' as many others had. Having arrived and feeling it was so meant I decided to take the risk and go with it and see what happened.

I managed to set my mobile phone alarm for 6.00am with the guidance of a co-worker, as my technology skills are very limited at times! I hardly had any energy to read the script that Brandon had given us when I returned to my holiday chalet, so instead decided to get to bed in preparation for my early start.

*How did **Lesson 22** relate to us in our life?*

Sometimes we will miss a golden opportunity by hesitating too long. This is where learning to listen to your intuition can be very helpful. If you feel drawn to do something but filled with doubts and questions, get out of your head and into your body.

Sit quietly and feel how your body is reacting to the thought of doing whatever it is. If it fills with excitement then your answer is clear. Your body never lies and always knows far better than your head. Your brain can play tricks but your body can't. I never doubt my body signals so if it is telling me it's ok and dare to take the risk, then I do.

However if your body feels panicky and negative at the thought of doing whatever it is, there is a reason, perhaps one that you are not as yet aware of. Sit with the feeling in your body and try to get to the core of the feeling. Is it fear or is it something different.

We all sense without always knowing and again our bodies have the ability to know before our brain.

Learn to listen to your body before responding to your thoughts.

I invite you to explore **Lesson 22** . . . .

Think of a time when you wanted to do something but didn't. What held you back, was it your thoughts or a reaction from your body. For the next week decide to listen to your body before acting on your thoughts when making any new decisions. Record what you do and see what the results are. You may well be surprised at how loudly your body speaks to you!

_____

_____

_____

_____

_____

_____

_____

_____

_____

_____

Sat 26th Feb 05

Luckily the alarm woke me and I crept out of bed and tried to get ready quietly and leave the holiday park without waking everyone, aware I was the only one getting up at that unsociable hour.

The day with Brandon was 'full on' from 7.15am–8pm.

Unfortunately for me as the day wore on I felt more and more weary. I wished I could feel more fired up, but I think the last week had caught up on me and I was finding this 'Journey work' very hard going.

However, it was lovely to connect with like-minded souls and I even saw one woman that I had met at Mana Retreat, in the Coromandel. I made new friends, which was very refreshing after spending so much time alone on my travels. I did an 'emotional journey' with one of the other trainers and she really went to pieces. I had support from one of the practitioners and we were with her for about 2 hours. That nearly finished me off, though it was so good to witness the process properly. By this time I had a dull headache so had some quiet time before retiring to bed in preparation for another 'heavy' day working with Brandon.

LESSON 23

RECOGNISING WHEN I'M IN THE 'RIGHT' PLACE

Even though I felt weary and vulnerable I knew I was in the right place. It was a 'knowing' with my body speaking louder than my mind.

How did Lesson 23 relate to us in our life?

Similar to lesson 22 we can learn to listen to the signals and know when we are in the right place with the right people at the right time.

*I invite you to explore **Lesson 23** . . . .*

Reflect when you have felt completely right about something/ somebody and try to remember why you did. Did it *feel* right or did you *think* it was right.

As you read on you will learn how I certainly acted on my body even though I felt scared to do so

Spend the next week identifying the difference between thinking and feeling and record it below.

_____

_____

_____

_____

_____

_____

_____

_____

Sun 27ᵗʰ Feb 05

Another early start at 7.15am starting with a meditation. I was so thankful when I realised today was going to be lighter and hopefully easier. It was good to reconnect with the other trainers and after the intensity of yesterday it had brought us all very close to each other. I only wished I had met some of these people at the beginning of my travels as I had some lovely offers to stay with them, but unfortunately there is no time left to do this now.

I worked with a lady on a 'physical journey' who had an issue with 25 people and seemed to be so much better with it all after her journey. There was so much evidence to show how powerful Brandon's emotional and physical journey was in healing at a cellular level. By the end of the day I saw and heard stories that showed healing had taken place. Her work is spreading universally and I was becoming more keen to use these tools myself when I returned home.

The day came to a crescendo finale and then Brandon took all of us trainers for an Indian meal. This was a lovely way to unwind and get to know each other properly. I went with Barry, who lived in Christchurch and we seemed to have a lot in common.

Brandon, her husband Kevin and Bill, her video/music man were all there and we shared different thoughts.

I felt the urge to tell Brandon how I had come on her intensive 5yrs ago and how it had influenced me into changing my whole life and now the amazing synchronicity of being in NZ the same time that she was visiting. My body crazed me to speak out but I struggled to do so in a room of strangers. However when she offered us the space to share anything, I knew that was the right time and stood up and thanked her for the privilege of being able to be part of her weekend and proceeded to tell her my story. As soon as I said my piece, my body calmed, it was happy that I had spoken the words I so wanted to share with Brandon. She had a dynamic energy and was totally passionate about her subject and that is why I feel so many are in awe of her.

Mon 28th Feb 05

LESSON 24

KNOWING THE DIFFERENCE BETWEEN 'FEELING RIGHT' AND 'SHOULD DO'

When I was preparing to leave my 'very basic' holiday stay I had such a surprise when I turned round and saw standing at my open door, Barry! 'Whatever are you doing here and how did you find me?' I asked.

He looked quite sheepish, 'I was wondering if you would like a guide for the next 2 days?'

I was completely stunned and didn't know how to answer. So many questions were going round my head and yet my instinct felt it would be lovely to share some of the travelling with someone for a change and have some company.

I decided to go with my 'gut' and accept his kind offer, despite the many unanswered questions. I guess this was truly a time when I trusted my intuition! The amazing thing was . . . . I had been feeling a bit lonely and thinking how good it would be to have some company on my travels!

First stop was at Barry's home, which was only 10mins away, to pick up a few belongings. As I was there I saw a photo of a woman and asked him if it was his wife. He nodded and then told me how she had died two and a half years ago with cancer and how they had been married 45 years. Barry was 19 years older than me and had experienced a very different life to me, but we soon realised that we had a lot of common ground.

Once his name was added to my car hire he took over the driving to give me a rest. It was good to be able to sit back and view the scenery without having to negotiate the roads at the same time.

Our first stop was the Botanic Gardens in Christchurch, which were very different to any gardens I had ever visited in Britain. We drove down Fendaldon, which was known as the no1 'posh' superb, and Barry pointed out the 'Black Box', which was a house, built by an architect, but how the plans for such an ugly building had been passed in such a beautiful area was beyond us both! It was horrendous and quite out of keeping with everything else in the area.

Next we headed east to the Queen Elizabeth II Park where the Commonwealth games had once been held. We visited the Gethsemane gardens, which had been created around the bible. The couple that owned it were now building a replica of 'The Ark' where they would eventually hoped to be holding reception parties. It was fabulous, and was completely made of wood; I would love to return to see the finished masterpiece.

We drove on to Lyttleton where all the surrounding rock was volcanic.

Barry drove down through Cashmere, the second largest suberb of Christchurch and then onto Hammer Springs where we arrived about 5.30pm. Feeling peckish we went to the local Tavern for a meal where I once again indulged in potato wedges (it's becoming a bit of a habit) but they are so tasty!

Barry stayed in my chalet as I had a spare bed and because he was such a gentleman I felt comfortable with his presence.

*How did **Lesson 24** relate to us in our life?*

Carl Rogers, the founder of Person Centred Counselling often talked about 'Conditions of Worth', meaning that we are so influenced by what we 'should' be and do that we forget who we really are. Daring to act on our own 'gut' instinct helps us to reconnect to the person deep inside and also shows how much we value ourselves. If we allow ourselves to act on our own feelings we will truly live a more peaceful life, even though we may not be pleasing everyone else.

I was influenced by what others may think if I allowed Barry to travel with me and then I realised that I was a long way from home and there was no one here that would even be interested. I also felt I was comfortable with this man even though I hardly knew him and felt we would be able to work out the more delicate side of 'how' we would stay with each other later.

I invite you to explore **Lesson 24** . . . .

Record when you have felt torn between what you 'want' to do and what you felt you 'should' do. What decision did you take and what was the outcome?

How do you feel now about the difference?

_____

_____

_____

_____

_____

_____

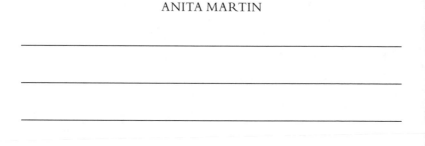

Tues 1st March 05

We were greeted by the coldest day I have yet had in NZ. It was also dull and grey and reminded me of home, but not the part of home I missed!

We went into Hammer Springs for lunch and really enjoyed tucking into toast with vegemite and cappuccino. It had been ages since I'd had a breakfast like that!

After satisfying my palette, we set off to Kaikoura and stopped to have crayfish chowder, which was also extremely tasty and filling. The weather was still cold as we moved onto Bleinheim, to be near the ferry for tomorrow. It was lovely having Barry's company, though I felt he might be reading more into it than I was, so I tried to very gently make it clear that this had no chance of developing into anything else. He understood and respected my feelings but it didn't change the fact that I was aware of his wishes. He stayed one more night as I had a spare room again and he had travelled so far by now that it made sense for him to return by ferry after I had gone.

Wed 2nd March 05

We drove to Picton, which was very near the holiday park and I was pleasantly surprised at the high quality of shops. I bought some gifts to take home and then we found a café that overlooked the harbour for coffee.

It was a much brighter day and I was so glad I would be leaving Barry in the sunshine. Finally the time came to say 'goodbye' to this Kiwi who had been such good company and I had grown very fond of. I knew that we would keep in touch and remain good 'pen-pals'.

I drove onto the ferry and we left Picton just after 12.30 for a 3hr journey and return to the North Island where I began this trip 4 weeks ago.

On the ferry I met a lovely young woman from Nelson, Denise, who ran a farm with her partner, sister and two children. We immediately connected and I gave her my e-mail as she was hoping one day to visit UK.

I drove to the holiday park that I stayed at when I went across the ferry 2 weeks ago.

I am now going to drive up the west coast to reconnect with Wendy who so kindly put me up at the beginning and pointed me in the right direction when I was a stranger to this beautiful country.

Thurs 3rd March 05

I set out at 9am for a long drive to New Plymouth. I soon felt the weariness creeping over me, just as I had before when I'd being trying to concentrate on the roads and look at the map at the same time. I stopped for coffee and again for lunch and still struggled, so at one point just pulled over for a 10mins catnap. It seemed to refresh me sufficiently to get me through the last part of the journey.

LESSON 25

ALLOW THE UNIVERSE TO TAKE CARE OF YOU

I arrived about 4.00pm and was very pleasantly surprised when I discovered that there was a swimming pool, heated and outdoor. My last night in a holiday park and what a bonus! I had so been asking for a swim and was delighted that at last I was going to get one.

*How did **Lesson 25** relate to us in our life?*

'Ask and it is given.' I really do believe those words just as I believe 'Careful what you ask for.' The universe has a way of looking after us if we allow it. Some would say it's God, others would name it something or someone else. I'm not exactly sure what or who I would name it but I do believe there is a much stronger force than us. I often throw a comment up and ask 'Whoever is there please guide me'. Sometimes I feel it is my dear father who died in 1996. In so many ways I feel his presence and by following my dream of writing I feel I'm achieving something he wanted to do also but didn't complete.

Why do I believe? Not because I've been told to but because I've experienced and heard from others so much evidence of a stronger power than us. So often when I have truly prayed and been open to receive, the answers have come, often in a bizarre way. The words I often use are 'Show me the way'. I believe if you are open to allowing the answers without attaching to the outcome, they will show themselves, but not necessarily as you expect.

*I invite you to explore **Lesson 25** . . . .*

Next time you are searching for an answer, throw your question up to the universe and then allow time for the answer to come and be aware that it may not come from a source you expect, so open your awareness around you, or you may miss it.

Sometimes the answers come in the most bizarre ways e.g. you may read something in a book, paper or a magazine. A friend may say something, give you something or it may be that you stumble over something. There are so many ways your answer may come to you, so just be aware as much as possible. Chances are if you miss the message the first time there will be another happening which will bring it to your notice.

Record your question below and then watch what happens.

_____

_____

_____

_____

_____

_____

_____

_____

_____

Fri 4th March 05

A slow start as despite waking early I felt I needed to take it slowly, so didn't rush and finally left the holiday park about 10.30am after surprising Mum with another phone call.

This is my last journey alone as tonight I will be with Wendy (from whence I came) and no longer have to cope with my solitude. I had a leisurely drive stopping on route as and when I felt like it and arrived at Wendy's about 4pm. It felt like 'coming home' as I approached Raglan, and I sensed the familiarity that you do when you retrace the steps you've walked before. Raglan, a huge favourite of mine, not just because it's where my adventure began, but for its uniqueness and wonderful energy. The buzz of the small village is alive with surfers and travellers. They spill out of the bars and restaurants, sharing tales of their experiences and mixing with like-minded souls as if they had known each other all of their lives.

LESSON 26

APPRECIATING & ACCEPTING

Allowing Wendy to spoil me supported me in my solo journey. It's important to allow others in and not always be too 'independent'.

When I arrived, Wendy was preparing my room downstairs where Bill had stayed on my last visit. I loved that room and now it was mine for the next 3 nights—I was thrilled. I so appreciated Wendy's warm hospitality.

It was so good to see Wendy and once again she welcomed me with open arms just as she had on that first day in New Zealand. The buzz began . . . we didn't know where to start as the wine was uncorked we delved into catching up. I was also greeted at Wendy's by a single rose sent by Barry with 'Bon Voyage, adien bjeh.' How touching and kind of him. I e-mailed him later to thank him.

Two of Wendy's friends joined us for a chat, Janet, who was on a very similar path to us, and Ruth, Wendy's partner in 'Sacred Journey's'. This was going to be a powerful weekend!

Later Wendy had a telephone conversation with Ross, a friend who lived nearby. Ross was paralysed from the chest down following a rugby injury when he was just sixteen years old; he was now in his 30's. He asked Wendy if I would do a Brandon Baye's 'Journey' with him. Having just recently been involved in the work with Brandon Bayes I felt quite comfortable to do this. A mutual time was made between us for next day and then Wendy and I spent the next 3½ hours discussing my journey around the South Island, with me showing off all the photos I'd taken. She enthusiastically shared my journey the 2nd time around.

*How did **Lesson 26** relate to us in our life?*

Sometimes we try to be too independent and we can miss receiving from those who want to give.

Appreciation is an important part of human relationships and it is good to recognise both when we need to show it and also when we need to accept what is being offered to us.

On my journey I learned to be grateful when others offered assistance be it in whatever way they chose. If I had refused the help when offered I would not only have missed out on so many wonderful moments but also denied others the opportunity to give. It can be very fulfilling to give to another so think twice before you deny others the chance to give to you.

*I invite you to explore **Lesson 26** . . . .*

Reflect when someone has helped you or given you something. How did you receive it? Did you show appreciation?

Make a note of next time this happens and record your reaction. Also record how they reacted to your response and write what you think they felt.

Is it easy to appreciate and accept? If it is not, explore why.

_____

_____

_____

_____

_____

_____

_____

_____

_____

Sat 5th March

LESSON 27

LEARN FROM OTHERS

What a day! Wendy had a friend called Ross, another Maori. He had been injured in a rugby accident when only sixteen years old and was now paralysed from the chest down. Now in his thirties, he had turned his personal tragedy into a total positive by starting a business called 'Backup New Zealand' which encouraged disabled people to take part in sport. He exuded positive energy and I immediately bonded with him. He asked Wendy if I would support him through a Brandon Bayes Physical Journey, which of course I agreed to. He allowed the process to work for him, releasing whatever needed letting go of. Ross is such a compassionate man, in touch with both his 'Ying' and 'Yang'. After his treatment Wendy joined us for lunch and we stayed till after 4.00pm—I was so gripped by our connection.

Ross showed me round his bungalow which had been adapted for his disabilities and as I walked round with him I noticed rugby pictures everywhere. My thoughts went to a Seamus, a friend back home who was a keen Rugby follower and had asked me to look out for any tickets that I might be able to get my hands on. At the time I thought it would be highly unlikely as I'm not a fan myself, so I asked Ross if he knew of any access to Rugby tickets as a friend back home was eager to follow the Lions when they come to New Zealand later in the year. He smiled and said there was a possibility and that he himself was looking for someone who would be prepared to accompany him as he also wanted to go and needed someone to assist him. My ears pricked up as I just knew Seamus would get on so well with him and I was sure he would have no problem accompanying Ross on the tour. I told Ross more about him and as the day wore on he assured me that he would try to get some tickets. I was so thrilled to have found a contact and couldn't wait to email Seamus and surprise him with the news.

Wendy and I moved on and called to see Ruth and Annie, a writer from UK who was single and travelling alone. She had sold up and put 'no finish' on her trip—Wow, is that not trusting your intuition!!

ANITA MARTIN

This evening the four of us had a meal in Raglan and it was wonderful to connect once again with like-minded souls after so much 'alone time' in the last three and a half weeks.

In bed at 2.00am—the one and only big social night, apart from the dinner with Brandon!

How did **Lesson 27** *relate to us in our life?*

We continuously learn from others if we allow ourselves to. Ross was an amazing young man who taught me so much. Being positive had meant he had found a bearable way to live his life and serving others had taken the attention from himself.

So often we can get caught up in 'Poor me' and yet it's so easy to see others worse off. We can move our attention away from our downfalls and before long we will be feeling more positive.

I invite you to explore **Lesson 27** *. . . .*

Write a 'Grateful list' and try to include at least 50 things you are grateful for. Before long you will be viewing your life differently.

_____

_____

_____

_____

_____

_____

_____

_____

_____

_____

Now write about one or two people you admire or you consider as your mentors. As you describe them decide what it is about them that makes them special in your eyes.

What have you learnt from them?

_____

_____

_____

_____

_____

_____

_____

_____

_____

_____

Sun 6th March 05

Amazingly, after my late night I still woke at 8.00am and felt refreshed as luckily didn't over consume on alcohol!

This was to be another very social day. First coffee at Aqua Velvet with Annie, Ruth and Wendy (the same place we were at last night)! Annie and I had lots in common, especially writing. She had given up her home to travel indefinitely—and I think I'm brave!!!

We went back to meet up with Trish and went to see a house that her and Bronwin might be interested in buying together. It stood up high with magnificent views. There are so many lovely places to live here with such wonderful views. We went to Raglan for a drink and then saw Ross again. The next thing I know is I'm being taken away with him and some friends to go abseiling. I wasn't sure about it all but it felt right, so I went with the flow. However I obviously wasn't meant to do it as there wasn't enough wind! It was good to see Ross again though.

Back to Wendy's where she had prepared a feast for a crowd of us (Trish, her son and 2 friends) Alexa, Ben, Wendy and me. The bubbly flowed for my send off. What a weekend!

I telephoned Linda to check she was still ok to pick me up at Heathrow, then off to pack.

Awesome time—has it changed me?

I guess I'll have to wait and see when I land in England! The cold weather will shock me, I know that much.

Mon 7th March 05

The day had finally arrived to start my long journey home. I was so thrilled that Wendy had insisted on taking me to Auckland airport. We took my hired car back to Hamilton on route and I discovered that I had travelled 3,000 miles, which amazed the staff! I have a feeling a lot of those miles were getting lost and finding my way back on route!!

Wendy drove me the rest of the way and she stopped at a Jade shop on the way, where I suspected she was up to something, which would be confirmed later!

Everything went very smoothly. I checked in and then we had a coffee and a sandwich.

I was sad to be leaving New Zealand and felt strangely apprehensive about returning.

As we said and embraced our goodbyes Wendy slipped an envelope into my hand and told me to open it later—which I did on the plane and found a lovely jade necklace with a card, which expressed very warm wishes inside from Wendy.

LESSON 28

ALLOW THE JOURNEY TO CONTINUE

On the plane I connected with a lovely 27-year-old Swedish girl sitting beside me. She had just been visiting a friend and discovered her friend had changed since she'd connected with God. My new friend continued to discuss with me how it had opened her up as well. She believed just as I do 'everything happens for a reason' and we had a beautiful journey together.

*How did **Lesson 28** relate to us in our life?*

I believe we never stop learning and life is one big journey. If we invest our energy in the journey and not worry about the outcome we will not miss the important lessons along the way. If we only focus on the outcome we will most certainly miss some wonderful opportunities to grow.

We all know people who resist change and through life have become bitter, hard and very serious. Personally I prefer to notice every bump along the highway and invite change into my life, knowing that it will bring me more glorious lessons. I also know that as I learn to accept and deal with each one without fear I will become stronger and in turn be more able to assist others on their individual journeys'.

So rather than become hard and bitter from life experiences I intend to become tough while maintaining a good sense of humour, another very necessary ingredient to survive life.

*I invite you to explore **Lesson 28** . . . .*

As you journey through life from this moment on, take time to pause and notice what is happening around you and to you. Try not to resist it, instead embrace it, even when it feels negative. By accepting that it is happening for a reason may help you not to deny it and instead try to learn from it.

Start by keeping a journal and record all the lessons you learn, maybe to begin with just aim for one each day. As you commit yourself to this exercise your awareness will widen and you will be surprised how you notice lessons that come into your life. Remember though, the value of them depends on what you learn from them. It also encourages us to look more positively at every situation we are faced with, so I invite you to try this for yourself and I promise you will be amazed at how you may start to view your world differently.

Try the exercise first . . . . record below any lessons you recognise that come into your life during the next week . . . .

_____

_____

_____

_____

_____

_____

_____

_____

_____

Leaving New Zealand was very emotional, as it had become a second home to me. In five weeks I'd made some real friends that I knew would stay with me for life. Kindred spirits who shared so much in how they felt and who had opened their arms and welcomed me in. All around the two islands I had experienced so many emotions from delight, vulnerabilities, joy, fear and sometimes sheer amazement at how the land had so simply talked to me.

The depth of the bush, with the chatter of the cicadas and undergrowth that beckoned me in, the dampness that surrounded me and rain that felt *so refreshing and welcoming after the severe heat of the sun. Such contrast enveloped and washed over me until I felt part of the native land. Even the birds would hover overhead as if they were following to be my guide should I lose my way.*

I felt so protected in every way, never feeling alone, yet more alone than I'd ever been in my life.

The mountains and scenic views had a different feel and story of their own. I would stop my car to allow myself to absorb the magnificence that surrounded me. The perfume of the sea, so clear and forever in charge of its land would talk in so many languages to all those that stopped to listen. The wind engulfed the trees and evidence of its strength was seen by some of the finer branches growing in one direction. It looked like a moving picture, which had been put on pause.

When driving I was once again made aware of how treacherous the mountain roads could be. The land cried out to be respected and if I didn't I was given a harsh lesson to remind me. Being a visitor I often learnt the hard way but at the end of five weeks I didn't need so much reminding.

Dear New Zealand you called me and opened your arms to welcome me in. I experienced so much of you in 3,000 miles of travelling and my journey has changed my life and it can never go back to where it was . . . forever moving on.

As the flight descended on my homeland I felt my energy change as I began to feel excited about seeing Linda, a familiar face, once again and going home to my 'sacred space' where comfort and security played a large part.

Adjusting to the temperature again may prove a bit of a challenge as I've become acclimatized to summer weather and would gladly continue to do so. At least I was returning to the onset of spring whereas New Zealand would soon be preparing for its autumn.

As I walked through the departure lounge, truly leaving New Zealand behind me I felt a new strength from all my travelling. I still may not have answers to all my questions but I do feel many will be revealed to me as a result from all that I have learnt as a 'lone traveller'.

Thank you New Zealand.

COINCIDENCES OR SYNCHRONICITIES

'Knowing'—Intuitively I know that I know best,
so I will stop being influenced by others

I don't believe in coincidences as I believe everything happens for a reason so my life has been filled with synchronicities.

I have arrived at this belief as a result of my own experiences and many that others have shared with me. In this chapter I will share with you some of those experiences . . . .

Everyday our lives are filled with synchronicities but many go unnoticed because unless our awareness is open to them they are often too subtle to catch our attention.

However when we do open up to them life takes on a whole new meaning. Just before I started writing this chapter I had a lovely example of how it manifests . . . .

I woke up to find a message on my telephone, one that I hadn't noticed was there the night before, after returning from an evening out. I was shocked when I listened to it, as it was from a friend telling me that he had heard another friend of mine had committed suicide. My first reaction was complete denial as is so often the case when we hear news like this so I decided to telephone this person who was supposed to have died, hoping desperately to hear his voice. When I heard the voice of an older woman I knew instantly it was true and sadly it was.

At that point I really wanted to talk to Dulce, a dear friend of mine, to share my feelings with her. However it happened to be her birthday so I didn't feel comfortable intruding on what I felt should be a joyful day with such sad news, so instead I sent her a text wishing her a happy birthday.

Later in the day I was travelling home on a park and ride bus and found tears were starting to surface and I longed for a hug from that same friend . . . . it was no coincidence that on stepping through my door I saw a parcel with her address on the back. She had sent a DVD of Billy Elliot and a card saying: 'Best Friends Hug the People They Love Every Day'.

I felt my prayer had been answered and to top it all I had only been talking to another friend the evening before and discussing 'Billy Elliot' and she had not seen it. Her passing words to me were 'I really must get that film'. I guess I knew where that DVD was going to be shared!

Every day in lots of ways synchronicities happen . . . .

I completely believe that we also have support from a higher source, even though I do not understand exactly how it works and I also believe that those who are no longer with us do try to contact us.

A few years ago Vince, a dear friend, died when climbing a mountain. Again the shock and sorrow I felt was overwhelming and then I experienced an incredible connection with him. One evening soon after hearing the news of his death I felt a great need to read one of his past emails. I became very frustrated when I couldn't find one but as I had an appointment I needed to leave, so closed down the computer and left. On returning later I found myself going straight to my computer, even though I never normally did this at such a late hour. There at the top of my inbox was an email from Vince. I felt a shiver all down my body, just as I always do when synchronicities happen.

Another time I knew Vince was near was when I woke one night feeling really anxious. I didn't know why and went to sit in my lounge to try and relax my body. It felt almost like a panic attack and took me a while before I calmed. Eventually I went back to bed and fell asleep.

When I woke in the morning I felt very calm and peaceful and was surprised after the experience I had in the early hours. I decided to have a soak in the bath and while I was lying there I was suddenly reminded of a dream I had after I went back to bed: I was on a train and Vince was sitting beside me. In my dream I knew it was his spirit and said to him 'Vince, do you think others know you are a spirit' He smiled and said 'No, they don't'. I touched him and he felt 'real' and it felt so good to be sitting beside him talking just as we used to for hours at a time.

I then sensed so strongly, as I lay there in the bath, that Vince had come to me that night to heal me. I really felt as if I had been in his company. How could I not believe in synchronicities?!!

Over the years I have learnt to trust my 'inner voice' and a wonderful example of that was when I gave my notice in at a job before I intended to!

I had been working as a Manager in a Residential Home for the elderly. Soon after starting I had told some of the staff that I felt I would be there about four years. Of course they were not convinced!

In my third year I became very restless and didn't feel I was coping with all the day to day happenings as I had previously been doing. I asked if it would be possible to reduce my hours to part time. At first my boss agreed but within days changed her mind saying she really felt she needed me to be a full time. I accepted her request to return to more hours and then completely surprised myself when within a week I heard myself giving my notice, even though I hadn't planned to!

They proceeded to ask me what notice I wanted and I answered 'Two months'. Again I was surprised at hearing my own voice and remember thinking 'That was quite sensible'. My inner voice had completely taken over and my trust in it had allowed it to be heard without questioning. I knew from that moment that there was a part of me that just 'knew' what was best for me and all I had to do was allow it to be heard and trust it.

What followed confirmed I had made the right decision . . . . I had a very strong sense that whatever I was meant to do next would show itself to me, but not in a way I expected. However because I'm 'human' I didn't always trust it enough and when it didn't happen as quickly as I wanted I started to look in the places I *sensed* were wrong. Of course nothing came from my panic search. I hunted the job pages and even went to few interviews, but each time ended up talking myself out of the opportunity of being offered the job. I couldn't quite get to grip with allowing the universe to do it for me even though I did believe it could. Applying it to me wasn't so easy. Then a breakthrough came that completely confirmed my beliefs forever . . . .

I was sitting at my breakfast table with a cup of coffee feeling quite anxious that nothing was happening, so decided to go through the telephone book and call a few Nursing Agencies and apply for some work that way. I knew from my body's reactions that hand's on nursing just wasn't where I was meant to be going but as I wasn't having any other signals coming my way I thought perhaps I'd better just bite the bullet and do something and it *felt* ok to make a few phone calls.

As I rang round I said the same 'spiel' to each one and then suddenly was surprised when one lady answered 'Haven't you just rung us?' I felt embarrassed and apologised 'Yes, quite likely, I'm sorry. I was ringing round all the agencies and must have called you back by mistake.'

Then she asked something that changed my whole direction *'Is this really what you want?'* I was stunned by her question and found myself being completely honest 'No, actually it isn't.'

'So what do you want?' Again surprised by her interest I answered, 'Actually I want to be a trainer.' 'And have you done training?' she continued.

I've everything I need to start but haven't found the opportunity to do it as yet'. I felt my energy changing as I talked with her. Adrenalin was rushing through me as if I sensed something very exciting was happening for me.

'That's very interesting' she said, 'I'm wanting to develop the training part of my business, so perhaps you should come and see me and bring your work so I can see what you've prepared'.

That was the start of a whole new chapter in my life which lead me to my 'life's work'. I worked for her for three months as a training co-ordinator and was then ready to fly on my own. From that moment on I have never doubted the quiet moments when I'm waiting to be shown the next step or path to take. I've learnt if I act through panic I will only have to start again.

Sometimes I've been surprised where my intuition has led me. I've even been led to work in a shop when my training went very quiet, which felt really strange but soon realised, as always that by working in that environment it was for reasons I was unaware at the time and I made new contacts which would naturally lead me to the next step of my journey.

Synchronicities are happening all the time and once we have become aware of them we start to notice them more. Looking back on my life I can identify them very easily . . . .

As a child I yearned to teach but ended up pursuing a nursing career. However many years later I re-connected with my desire to teach when I became a trainer. It is no surprise to me that being a trainer always felt more comfortable than being a nurse, even though I found that too very rewarding.

Nothing is wasted and everything is meant so when I began to train care and nursing staff I understood why being a nurse was a very relevant part of my journey.

Often we do not understand why something is happening and that is because we do not see or know the bigger picture, but later when you reflect back on your life you can often recognise why each experience had to happen to lead you to the next one.

If you are to believe, as I do, that we are here to learn lessons, it makes even more sense. So many times I've heard 'Why do I keep repeating the same mistakes' or 'I always seem to be attracted to the same type'.

Until we learn to recognise the lessons we are supposed to be learning, how can we move on from them?

Angie, a dear friend of mine was a well qualified caterer but she was feeling frustrated that work had dried up and was also concerned about her back causing her problems when she had worked many demanding hours. One day she decided to ring round (just as I did with the agencies) to see if she could find more employment, even though, just like me, she did not feel enthusiastic about it. While talking to a gentleman from a catering establishment she was surprised when he said 'Are you sure that's what you want, it's not well paid and it's hard work.' 'But it's all I know' was Angie's timid reply. 'Well you have a very good telephone voice so maybe you could do that type of work.' Angie thought no more about it until later her son rang to ask if she would consider doing telephone work for him as he felt her voice would be more accepting to the general public than the woman he was currently using. Angie was stunned and soon recognised what I meant by synchronicities!

PEOPLE COME INTO YOUR LIFE FOR A REASON

Response—I cannot change exterior force but
I can change my response to it.

People come into your life for a reason, a season or a lifetime.

When you figure out which it is, you know exactly what to do.

When someone is in your life for a REASON, it is usually to meet a need you have expressed outwardly or inwardly.

They have come to assist you through a difficulty, to provide you with guidance and support, to aid you physically, emotionally, or spiritually. They may seem like a godsend and they are.

They are there for the reason you need them to be.

Then, without any wrong doing on your part or at an inconvenient time, this person will say or do something to bring the relationship to an end.

Sometimes they die. Sometimes they walk away.

Sometimes they act up or out and force you to take a stand.

What we must realise is that our need has been met, our desire fulfilled, their work is done. The prayer you sent up has been answered and it is time to move on.

When people come into your life for a SEASON, it is because your turn has come to share, grow, or learn.

They may bring you an experience of peace or make you laugh.

They may teach you something you have never done.

They usually give you an unbelievable amount of joy.

Believe it, it is real, but only for a season.

LIFETIME relationships teach you lifetime lessons; those things you must build upon in order to have a solid emotional foundation.

Your job is to accept the lesson, love the person/people (anyway); and put what you have learned to use in all other relationships and areas of your life.

It is said that love is blind but friendship is clairvoyant.

Thank you for being a part of my life.

In the early days of running my business, I was given the above words(author unknown) and they had a profound effect on me and many others since that I've passed them on to. For the first time in my life I understood the value of not attaching, but instead of allowing my life to flow as it naturally needed to.

I began to see my life as a journey and not a destination that I had to arrive at and once there, maintain. So many times in my life I had tried to control a situation or another person, so I could have a better outcome, only to be very disappointed when I couldn't and then had to deal with the consequences as well as my ever plummeting self esteem. Does this ring any bells with you? I know it has with the many people I've shared it with through my work as a trainer.

As soon as I viewed my purpose for being here differently, my view of my life and those in it changed as well. It made complete sense to me that we are here to learn lessons and by doing so we need other people to be in our life in order to complete these lessons. I also recognised how I had repeated some lessons many times until I changed the way I dealt with them and then I no longer had that particular lesson present itself to me.

It was like an awakening when I recognised how I would never feel my own power if I searched for change in others and not in myself. As I now so often tell others 'You can't change others, but you can change yourself and by changing yourself others will most likely change anyway, as you are dealing with them differently, therefore they will not respond as they did before. Putting this into practise really did change my life and my self esteem grew very quickly.

To feel empowered and value yourself are two very attractive qualities and when you have accomplished them you will naturally attract others who have learnt the same lessons as like attracts like . . . . When you truly value yourself you will be able to value others in a healthy way too.

No one likes being with a needy person for too long, as they suck energy from us and as a result we feel drained. When we are feeling needy we are often not conscious of it and therefore don't intentionally act in this way, but due to the very nature of how we are feeling we cannot help ourselves.

A good example of this is 'Meeting a new potential partner'. When we are initially attracted to someone and then have the opportunity to go out with them, we are often excited at the prospect of the date becoming a relationship. If we don't allow the universe to work it out for us we can try to take control of the situation by perhaps showing more enthusiasm than perhaps the other person is ready for. If we then get caught up in our need we then become less aware of the other person and may not pick up the signals that are coming our way. Hence our 'need' is interpreted as 'needy' and as soon as the other person feels pressured to respond and any attraction they may have felt will be diminished as they will now feel they have lost their power. There is nothing more attractive than not quite knowing if the other person is feeling like you. The mystery of not knowing is demonstrating a person who is comfortable in their own skin and someone who is not going to drain you of all your energy. As soon as we feel pulled, under pressure or worse still pursued, the dynamics change.

This does not mean that a man should not 'woo' a woman, it's the way it's done that matters. A friend of mine once said, 'I feel I've always been pursued which has never felt comfortable as it feels like a control thing, however to be wooed would be lovely.'

I'm inclined to agree with this. To show you are interested but allow the other person time to see if they feel the same, is fine. If they show they are not feeling the same attraction then that is the time to accept it wasn't meant or maybe it's the wrong time. If we try to change their mind by acting in a certain way, it is very unlikely to change anything, but more likely to make you now look slightly desperate!

People come into our lives for so many reasons: to help us learn, to give us joy, to offer support at maybe a time when we really need it, to introduce us to something or someone new or maybe to provide us with a lesson. Whatever reason it is they are there for a purpose and if we recognise it, we learn how to deal with them. Often we don't recognise the reason until they are taken out of our life, but that is because when we are immersed in the lesson, so cannot always see beyond it and it's not until much later that we can identify it.

However what we can do is just accept that it is a lesson, even if we don't know what the lesson is at that time. All will come clear eventually, all you are meant to do is experience it and use your intuition to do this.

This is another reason why developing your intuition is so valuable, as you will learn to recognise signals from your body, rather than your mind of what to do or how to act. These signals are your most important ones as your body never lies, but your mind can play tricks and convince you of things you want rather that what is best for you.

When you meet a new person or go into a new situation your body will talk loud and clear and depending on how much you have learnt to listen to it you will know how to respond. Sometimes we do recognise repeat lessons very quickly, but still feel the urge to repeat them, knowing the outcome will probably not be positive. This is often because we did not complete the lesson before so are given the opportunity to do it differently. It can take many tries at the same lesson, with either the same person or maybe even different people before we truly feel we don't need that lesson again!

It's very empowering when we do recognise our own growth and can avoid the same mistake from a place of knowing.

As we empower ourselves, the view of our world changes too. I no longer look for someone else to 'make' me happy. I remember my counselling tutor, many years ago responding to my statement 'But, he makes me so angry'. He replied 'No one makes you angry

Anita, they do what they do and you have a choice of how you respond.' My first reaction was denial and anger at my tutor for suggesting it was my fault if I felt angry. However, with some careful reflection I became aware of how true his response was and so learnt another powerful lesson. Sometimes lessons are painful but the growth we feel after can feel like an awakening.

I'll give you some examples of lessons I learnt . . . .

When I was nursing I found myself looking after a patient who happened to be an author, who worked at Bush House, London. As soon as I discovered his profession I felt a connection with him, as I had loved writing since a child. One day he asked if I had any hobbies, so I shared with him my interest and he asked if I would share any of my writing with him. I realised I had been asking for exactly what he was offering . . . . 'some feedback from an experienced writer'. However my ego was very nervous as my confidence was low where my writing was concerned and I felt anxious that any rejection I received may result in losing my desire to write, which I knew would devastate me. I reflected for a while and knew that I would regret it if I didn't take this opportunity to have my work scrutinised by a stranger, albeit an expert. So I selected some of my work and gave them to him. It was like waiting for an exam result. Several days later, he asked if I would like feedback. 'Of course' I replied, though not sure I meant it. He then proceeded to talk me through each piece that I had submitted and gave me some very constructive comments. He told me my style of writing was good and that life's experience would add to the content. He then offered me support in getting some work published and I felt thrilled at the prospect as at nineteen years old I hadn't even dreamt I would be 'good enough' to venture down that path.

As a result, after he left the hospital he kept in touch and helped me to pursue my dream and I had some articles published abroad, as his work was mostly involved with foreign countries. Gradually life pulled us apart and looking back I realised he came along to teach me to value my passion and to understand that it is possible to have dreams come true, I just had to believe in them. I have never doubted it since and as a result I went on to create and run a patient's magazine, and gained so much joy from not only having my own work published every month but also giving other aspiring writers a chance too.

When my partner, Tom, was turning 50 I wanted to give him a special gift. He had always wanted to visit New York and I wanted so much make that possible. However my left brain was giving me all the reasons why I 'shouldn't', 'It's too much money', I will take forever to pay it back' . . . .

When I shared it with my work colleagues they responded 'You just have to do it, it's once in a life time'. My intuition spoke loud and clear 'Just do it, all will be ok.' So I decided to trust and go ahead.

Then about a week before we were due to leave I was standing in my kitchen one morning and heard the post being delivered. I retrieved the envelopes and returned to the kitchen where I began to investigate what was in them. I opened one of the envelopes and to my surprise a cheque escaped from my hand and floated across the floor landing a few feet in front from me. I thought it was one of those promotional cheques which had no value, but then I noticed a solicitor's letter still in the envelope. I had been left £5,000 in a will, by a relation of an elderly lady I had looked after and who had died a few years ago. The relation had now died and had remembered me in her will. I was stunned and the timing was perfect. Now I could go to New York, knowing that I could comfortably afford it!

The reason the cheque came after me booking the trip was so I would learn the lesson of 'trusting my intuition' first. This is a lesson I've had many times and each time I think I will be more relaxed about it only to be tested yet again! I guess there are some lessons that follow us through our lifetime. I know with all my heart that if I keep fine tuning my intuition and listen to my body and not my mind, it will get easier and it has but I can't afford to become complacent so I like the fact I keep getting 'wake up' calls to check where I am with my trusting. Never forget we are 'human' though, it helps to keep us grounded and understand that we were meant to make mistakes.

Another good example of using my intuition . . . . I was working as a Manager in a Residential Home for the elderly. Having trained as a counsellor and trainer I knew in my heart it was time to move away from the residential setting and time to pursue where I felt I was being lead, running trainings and practising as a Counsellor. My left brain, once again challenged at the prospect of change whereas my right brain as always welcomed it with open arms, so it felt like quite a conflict for me to deal with. I decided to take small steps and asked my boss if I could reduce my hours to part time. At first she agreed and told me to take two days off to chill, as she sensed I was tired and on overload. Within 24 hrs she asked to meet with me. Hardly enough time to chill, I thought, but I agreed and as soon as we sat down she told me that unfortunately she couldn't accept my part time request as the post really did need full time and she didn't want it to become a job share. My immediate response was to 'people please' and so let my left brain have a voice and told her I would continue as before. As I left her I was aware of my entire body feeling uneasy and negative.

Within two days of returning to work I asked for a meeting, knowing she was returning home, abroad. I had no idea why I'd asked for a meeting, only aware I needed to talk to her. Once seated with a coffee in my hand I announced 'I need to give my notice in.' No one was more surprised than me to hear those words! I had no idea I was going to say what I did, but it *felt* so right!

My boss actually looked less surprised than I felt and told me she had sensed I needed to move on but just wanted to deny it as long as possible, knowing it would create another job for her, in having to replace me.

My right brain had been allowed a voice and it rejoiced in being heard. As a result my body relaxed and for the first time in a few days I felt in tune again, even though I didn't know where it was all going to lead . . . . I didn't need to!

How often do we have similar experiences with relationships? Knowing a certain person may not be good for us and yet finding ourselves hanging onto them anyway. Even finishing it and then re starting it many times before we can truly walk away. That is an example of our right and left brain truly in conflict. Fear steps in and hugely influences us making it even more difficult to trust our intuition. There is no easy answer but I do know by learning more and more about how intuition works it does become easier to follow it. One way I visualise it is by imagining the sea when it is rough with waves disturbing the tranquillity of the water. If you were surfing on them it would be a lot easier to go in the same direction than try and surf against them. Yes it would still be difficult and even scary but not anywhere near as frightening as trying to go against them. Life is a journey and at times can feel like those waves in the sea, but if we stay focused and grounded and ask for support we will be given the tools we need to 'ride the storm'. We were never promised that life would be easy, but it can certainly be a lot more comfortable if we learn to go with it rather than against it.

Perhaps now would be a good time to explore those that you have allowed into your life and see if you can recognise the lessons they have taught you. Remember it does not always mean harsh lessons; they may have come to show you joy and healing. Perhaps you need a bit of help on 'self value' as it will feel much more of an uphill struggle if you don't value yourself. Why not enrol on a class or invest in some 1-1 to help you help yourself before you change things that you know are going to test you.

Whatever you decide to do, just know that you have the control button, whenever you decide to use it. When we feel empowered, our whole life can change. Until we learn to stop blaming others for our circumstances we will never feel in that place, so start at the most important place—yourself.

EMBRACING THE NOW

*Lessons—when I feel hurt from the past I will look
for the lesson and learn from it.*

I felt a good way to finish my book would be to 'embrace the now'. As that is all there is and always will be. While we spend energy on questioning our past and trying to work out our future we miss the most important time of all—NOW.

Of course if we spent all our time in the now we wouldn't plan anything, so naturally like all things, a balance is called for. When it comes to our past though, regrets have no use in our life and will only cause us more pain, so acceptance is needed in order to move on and allow ourselves to grow further. Acceptance is the most important gift we can give to ourselves.

Perhaps we didn't always do all what we now feel we could have done, but we need to remember that when we were experiencing whatever it was, we were not the person we are now. We so often judge ourselves from where we are now and not from where we were then. Every day brings more growth so why would we deal with things now in the same way as before? Once we understand how our growth, however subtle it may be to us, changes our thoughts, reactions, choices, feelings and ultimately our decisions, we will be more accepting of how we have lived in the past.

With all this in mind, it is only natural that when we reflect on our past we will question all those things, but so often with a harsh judgement, instead of a gentle acceptance of maybe 'Haven't I grown since then' or 'at least I know that I don't need to experience those things again, as I've learnt how to deal with them differently.'

How often have you used the words 'If I could do it all over again I would . . . . ' Well you can't, so what's the point in wasting good energy on something you have no control over and can't change, when it could be used in the present moment and even possibly the future.

Many of us miss daily miracles that go on right under our nose because our thoughts and attention are somewhere else. Bringing our awareness into the 'now' can change our life forever. Instead of *existing* through each day, try allowing distractions to take you to wherever they lead you and you will begin to notice a different quality of living. Of course this isn't always possible, especially when you are needing to be focused at work. However you can allow moments of doing it, say in your lunch time when you want to chill, even if it is for a short while. If you do allow yourself these moments your intuition will wake up and you will begin to dare to act on it with amazing results . . . .

When I was working in a Nursing Agency I had a very strong desire to go out at lunch time to a charity shop and buy a long navy skirt. It's as if I knew one would be there! I didn't question it but instead just did it and amazingly found a really good quality one in my size. It wasn't until I was back at work and sitting at my desk that I reflected on just how astonishing it all was. I love the saying *'Get out of your own way'* it really makes me think—yes, I am so often my biggest block!

If you start living in the 'Now' you will certainly experience less stress, which in itself will give you a more comfortable way of living and life will become more colourful as you notice details that you didn't before.

This all sounds very easy in theory but of course just like learning anything new it doesn't usually come naturally especially if you have never done it before. So how can you begin to live more in the 'now' . . . .

Accept that it may not be easy and give yourself permission to mess up sometimes, knowing that you can try again.

Let's approach it as if you were learning a foreign language. Would you expect yourself to speak fluently after a week of learning? I don't think so. You would start by knowing that it wouldn't come naturally as it's completely new to you. Having the understanding that practise would be necessary to improve, will help you be more patient with yourself.

Begin . . . . by allowing yourself some 'me' time—without it you are not even going to get started. Make sure it's time that you can comfortably give yourself. If you are a very busy person who has never considered anything so luxurious as having 'time out just for you', then maybe just 10mins to start with is all you feel you can allow yourself. Don't worry, as you learn to experience this different way of living 'Me time' will move up your priority list.

Next . . . . think of something that gives you pleasure— maybe a walk in the country, a soak in the bath, reading a good book, enjoying a tasty meal, anything that you truly look forward to doing. If you can't think of anything it may be because you simply haven't allowed yourself time before, so think of something that you would like to do, just for you. You will know when you have discovered it because you will either feel a slight regret that you haven't allowed yourself time to do it previously or it will remind you of when you have done it and reflecting on it will reconnect your feelings to the experience.

Now comes the tricky part, making it happen . . . . somewhere in your busy schedule you need to find a place to slot 'Me time' in, but as I previously said, be realistic and don't give yourself more time than you are initially comfortable with, even though in your heart you probably could do with it.

Even if its 10mins to allow yourself to sit down with a cuppa looking at a magazine, that's fine, you have at least started.

When you are ready to experience this quality time, make sure you have disconnected yourself from any distractions, which means turning off telephones and getting away from other people, as there is no point in doing this if you know there is a chance that you could be disturbed.

When I decided to start taking some 'time out' in the evening from my family and residents, as living in my job made it very important to find a space for me, I would take a glass of perfectly chilled wine and disappear to have a soak in the bath. I would tell my family what I was going to do and make it very clear that I was not to be disturbed unless there was an emergency. Initially they didn't quite get the message and would come and bang on the bathroom door but insistence on my part soon got the message through and before long they accepted without question that they did not disturb Mum at those times.

I have since realised that from valuing myself my daughter has truly learned to value her time, even though her role as mummy is very demanding. As a role model I demonstrated to her how looking after me did not mean I loved her less. I was a much better mother to her because I wasn't always drained from giving to others without considering my needs. Of course I learned some of these lessons the hard way just as many others have, but at least

I learnt them and acted on them before she reached adulthood so she was still influenced by me enough to hopefully learn her own valuable lessons. Allowing ourselves 'quality time' definitely shows us where we are on 'self value'. As I so often quote 'You can't look after others if you don't look after yourself first.' In order to be there for those you love and care for you really need to invest in your own self care first or you will soon feel emotionally and physically drained. This especially applies to those working in the care profession. To go home and carry on with the caring role just cannot work successfully if you have not considered your own welfare first.

Embracing the 'Now' helps us to focus on what really matters. If we don't invest in the present moment what sort of future are we preparing for ourselves or our children.

Fear is created from:

Faulty

Evidence

Appearing

Real

If we feed the fear it will become our reality because that's how manifestation works. If we believe long enough that something will happen, it will. The universe responds to the energy of what we *focus* on. This has been proved scientifically many times and if you want to explore this subject more I would suggest you read David Hamilton's books on the subject 'It's The Thought That Counts' and 'How the Mind Can Heal The Body' two of many others that he has also written. David has researched the subject and is an inspirational speaker and I would go as far as to say one of my mentors.

I also know from my vast experiences how true it is as I have been amazed at how my thoughts have become my reality. However focusing on 'Now' helps us not to invite fear in as we are not allowing our thoughts to stray into the unknown or imagine what 'might be'. To manifest positive events into your life allow yourself to dream and when you have a negative thought try not to feed it but instead let go of it and bring your thoughts back to the present.

Mindfulness is a great way of getting in touch with the present moment. Why not try this exercise:

Pick up an object and for five minutes totally focus on it and see how much you can take in about it. Sometimes people find writing down what they observe helps them to remain focused. After five minutes, reflect on how much attention you gave the object and question yourself 'Did you think of anything else as well? With practise you can learn to focus more and more and learn to enjoy the quality of living, thinking and feeling in the moment.

When we spend time with people who have a lot of negative energy we often absorb it from them. Depending on where our energy is and how we are physically and emotionally will determine how porous we are to absorbing others negative energy.

As a nurse I had to learn how to give with compassion without depleting myself of the energy required for other patients and also have enough left at the end of the shift for me. When I was training I was very fortunate to have very caring tutors and one thing that was said to me will stay with me forever: 'If someone dies and you feel nothing, get out of nursing'. My dilemma was how would I do that? I devised my own theory 'Nursing is like walking a tight rope, if you fall one way you have gone in too far and got too involved. If you fall the other way you haven't allowed yourself to 'feel' enough. The only place is to be balanced on the tight rope. It isn't easy but who said it was meant to be?!! As a trainer I often quote those words and say how with practise we learn to walk the tight rope and it is definitely the only place that you will truly feel the rewards of the profession.

Learning to be in the 'Now' with patients also meant I gave much more quality care. Learning to let go after caring for them was just as important as giving my total attention when I was attending to them.

As a counsellor I know the value of giving all my attention when I'm with a client and after they leave I visualise their issues leaving with them. It is the only way to truly give to others without being drained yourself.

If we learn to compartmentalise our life it becomes easier to value what is happening right now. Allow a time and space for each event as much as possible. Of course there will always be unexpected events and traumas that take your attention when you least expect it, but if you have learnt to be more focused you will be able to deal with these unpredictable happenings with more energy and attention as well.

CONCLUSION

I would like to think that if and when I reach old age I will have created good, fond memories to reflect on. That won't happen if I never invest in the 'now'. If I'm constantly regretting or procrastinating over the past or fearful of the future I will prevent myself having memories that I would later want to revisit. Another reason to invest in the present moment!

As I bring this book to a close I ask you to really value every minute of your life and understand that it wasn't necessarily meant to be an easy ride but your perception and approach will make all the difference. I do not have 'bad' days anymore, I have 'challenging' ones and viewing them in this way has helped me to deal with them more positively.

Listening to my inner voice has truly allowed me to live in this wonderful space. A quiet mind will not only give you peace but will also allow you to become creative and playful and by practising this you will get in touch with your intuition—the most powerful way to live.

ABOUT THE AUTHOR

Anita Martin welcomes the opportunity to provide talks on her inspirational journey around New Zealand when she will share the value of the 28 lessons she learnt on Developing Intuition

Anita is also available for talks, trainings and workshops on the following subjects:

Developing Your Intuition
Anxiety Management
Building Self Esteem & Confidence
Improving Communication Skills
The Power of Writing
Starting Over
Grief & Bereavement
The Power of Laughter
Wellbeing for Body & Mind
The Power of Living in the Now

RESOURCES

Also by Anita Martin:

Relaxation & Visualisations CD—which will help you quieten your mind and relax your body, which is essential for developing your intuition

Developing Intuition Cards—a portable set of cards taken from the 28 lessons in the book.

Recommended Reading:

I have found the following Authors and books particularly inspirational and helpful in guiding me to find my own 'inner voice'.

Sonia Choquette—The Psychic Pathway
            Trust Your Vibes
            Your Heart's Desire

Brandon Bayes—The Journey

David Hamilton—It's The Thought That Counts
Destiny vs Free Will
How Your Mind Can Heal Your Body
Why Kindness Is Good For You
The Contagious Power Of Thinking

Julia Cameron—The Artists Way

Susan Jeffers—Feel The Fear And Do It Anyway

Eckhart Tolle—The Power of Now

Anita allowed her intuition to lead her on a journey of self discovery . . . .

As a Counsellor and Trainer, she shares with you how her life changed when she learnt to listen to her 'inner voice'

Her life has been full of synchronicities and she will help you to identify yours.

She invites you to join her on her solo trip to New Zealand where she identified 28 lessons she experienced along the way and by recognising and learning from each one she became more aware of her intuition. Anita encourages you to use her experiences as a lesson on developing your own intuition too.

Learning how to change her thought patterns changed her life! She had already made major changes in her life and felt more in tune with her destiny but now began to take much bigger steps toward achieving it. The journey became exciting and the more she trusted her intuition the more fulfilled she became.

The synchronicities that happened, the people she met, the places she visited were all part of the bigger picture . . . and she knew she was not necessarily meant to know the reasons why . . . 'all we need to do is experience what is happening now and not force the outcome, everything will be revealed when the time is right.'

Share Anita's journey and follow her tips on how to listen and act on your own 'inner voice' so you can manifest your dreams into reality.